DEVOTIONS
FOR
Little Boys and Girls

OID TestaMeNt

by Joan C. Webb

art by Joanne Vavrek McCallum

STANDARD
PUBLISHING
Cincinnati, Ohio

Unless otherwise noted, Scriptures are taken from the *International Children's Bible, New Century Version*, copyright © 1983, 1986, 1988 by Word Publishing, Dallas, Texas 75039. Used by permission.

Library of Congress Cataloging-in-Publication Data

Webb, Joan C., 1948-
    Devotions for little boys and girls / by Joan C. Webb : art by
Joanne Vavrek McCallum.
        p.   cm.
    Contents: [1] New Testament — [2] Old Testament.
    ISBN 0-87403-682-8
    1. Bible—Devotional use—Juvenile literature. 2. Children—
Prayer-books and devotions—English. 3. Bible games and puzzles—
Juvenile literature. 4. Devotional calendars—Juvenile literature.
 [1. Prayer books and devotions.] I. McCallum, Jodie, ill.
II. Title.
BS617.8.W43 1992
242'.62—dc20   91-37705
                                          CIP
                                              AC

ISBN 0-87403-681-X

Table of Contents

Dear Parents,

When my son and daughter were young, I searched for a book that I could read to them each night. I wanted the book to have short, simple stories based on biblical concepts. I wanted contemporary illustrations for the stories; pictures the children could identify with. My desire was to help them learn how the God-given truths of the Bible related to their lives. Although I did not find exactly what I wanted, I continued to read and adapt existing books and stories to our family's specific needs.

Devotions for Little Boys and Girls is an outgrowth of my original search. It is a daily Bible story devotional book for you and your child. It is designed to help you, the parent, guide your child in understanding God's love for him or her through His Son, Jesus, and His written Word, the Bible. Each story begins with a verse to think about and concludes with follow-up in the form of questions, suggested activities, and a prayer. Many of the simple activities encourage quiet learning times with your child. For active interaction, perhaps the following day, you may wish to do the more involved suggested activities.

This book is intended for young children three to six years old. Each devotion is complete on one page. You may write your child's name on the blank provided within the devotion. In this way, the book becomes uniquely individual. To encourage further participation, you may have your child draw a happy face or place a sticker at the top of the page to celebrate completing each story and/or activity (suggested stickers, Happy Heart Miniatures-#22-01375 or Children's Face Miniatures-#22-01386 by Standard Publishing).

I recommend that you hold or touch your child as you read to him or her, making this daily time a loving, sharing experience. Have fun!

Joan C. Webb

WHAT DID GOD MAKE?
GENESIS 1:1-13

It is by faith we understand that the whole world
was made by God's command. *Hebrews 11:3*

_____, a long time before you were born, God
was alive. He was alive before Mommy and Daddy were born. Even
before Grandma and Grandpa were born, God was alive.

But He was alone. There were no animals. There were no people.
There were no trees or flowers. Everything was dark.

But then God said, "Let there be light." And light came in the new
sky that God made. Then God made the earth and filled it with dirt
and water.

God looked at what He had made, and He said, "This is good. I like
what I see."

He put grass, trees, and seeds into the dirt. Up came flowers—
daisies, tulips, and roses. Up came vegetables—beans, corn, lettuce.
Apples, oranges, and bananas grew on the trees.

God looked all around Him.

"I am so happy with what I have made," He said. "This is good."

Questions:
1. Who was alive long before anyone else was born? (God)
2. What did God make? (light, sky, dirt, water, grass, trees, flowers,
vegetables, fruit)
3. What did God say? ("This is good. I am happy with what I
made.")

Activities:
1. Name two fruits and two vegetables that you like to eat.
2. Draw a picture of an apple tree. Color the apples red. Count the
apples on your tree.

Prayer:
Dear God, I know that You made the grass, trees, and all the veg-
etables and fruit. Thank You for making them for me to eat and enjoy.
Amen.

WINTER, SPRING, SUMMER, AND FALL
GENESIS 1:14-19

*Both the day and night are yours.You made the sun and the moon.
You created summer and winter. Psalm 74:16, 17*

_____, can you name the four seasons? I will
help you. They are winter, spring, summer, and fall. It is God who
made these different times of the year. God made the sky and the
earth. Then He put the sun and moon in the sky. The sun comes in the
day to give bright light. The moon comes at night to give a little light.
The sun and the moon help to give us the different seasons of the
year.

In the winter, it can be cold. Sometimes it snows. It is fun to play in
the snow. In the summer it may get hot. At night we can lie in the
grass and watch the stars.

God made the stars. People for many
years have liked looking at the twinkly
stars on a clear night.

Once again, God said, "This is good. I
like what I have made. I like the seasons
of winter, spring, summer, and fall."

Questions:

1. What are the names of the four seasons or times of the year that God made?
(winter, spring, summer, and fall)

2. What two kinds of light shine in the sky at night time? (the moon
and the stars) What gives light in the day time? (the sun)

Activities:

1. Sing together "Twinkle, Twinkle Little Star."

2. PARENT: Write the names of the four seasons on a piece of
paper, then invite your child to draw one thing that reminds him(her)
of each season. Examples: winter—snow, coats; spring—flowers,
green grass; summer—swimming, gardens; fall—playing in colorful
leaves, children going to school.

Prayer:

Dear God, we like the snow in winter and the flowers in the spring.
We like to go swimming in the summer, and we like the "crunchy"
leaves in the fall. Thank You for all four times of the year. Amen.

THE FIRST ANIMAL FARM
GENESIS 1:20-25

Lord, you have made many things—creatures large and small.
Psalm 104:24, 25

_____, do you like to watch animals? It's fun to listen to all the different sounds they make, isn't it? I want to tell you a story about the first animals.

God put trees and vegetables in the ground. Then He made animals to walk around and eat them. He put water in the lakes and rivers and oceans. He filled them up with fish. He made the little sunfish and the dolphins and the great big whales. He put singing birds in the tree tops. He made the cows, horses, pigs ,and chickens. He made the puppies and the kitty cats, the woolly lambs, and the cotton-tail bunnies. God even made the worms, frogs, turtles, and ladybugs.

It was a *very* big farm. God listened to the sounds of the many animals. He watched them walk and fly and swim.

After God made all the animals, He looked at them and said, "This is good. I like these animals I have made."

Questions:

1. What did God put into the lakes and rivers and oceans? (water and fish)

2. What did God put into the tree tops? (birds)

3. What did God make to walk on the earth? (many kinds of animals and bugs)

Activities:

1. Pretend you are visiting a farm. Take an imaginary walk through the trees, hills, and by the water. Name the animals and imitate the sounds that each one makes.

2. Sing "Old McDonald Had a Farm." (Change the words to "God the Creator had a farm.")

Prayer:

Dear God, You made all the animals, fish, and birds. Help me to take good care of all that You made. Amen.

ADVENTURES IN THE GARDEN
GENESIS 1:26; 2:8, 15, 18-25

But when God made the world, he made them male and female.

Mark 10:6

God was happy with all the animals and the birds and the fish that He made. But who would care for them and feed them all? God had a special plan.

"Let's make a man who can think, talk, and feel," said God. "He will take care of the birds, the fish, and all the animals. I will name him Adam."

Adam lived on the first farm. It was a beautiful garden farm called Eden. It had tall green trees and juicy red apples and yummy yellow bananas. Adam and the animals enjoyed living there.

God asked Adam to name each animal, fish, and bird. So Adam gave some animals short names like owl or ant or cow or cat. To others he gave longer names like octopus or elephant or butterfly.

_____, can you find the butterfly in the picture? Can you tell me what Adam named the other animals that you see in the picture?

One day God said, "Adam, I think you need a helper-friend. I will make someone to talk and work and live with you." So God made a woman to be Adam's friend, helper, and wife. Adam was very happy. He named his new wife and friend, Eve. Adam and Eve worked and lived together on the garden farm. They cared for all that God had made. Everything was perfect.

Questions:
1. Who named the animals? (Adam)
2. What were some of the names that Adam gave to the animals?
3. What was Adam's wife's name? (Eve)

Activities:
1. Name kinds of seeds that you could plant in your garden (ideas: carrots, beans, marigolds).
2. Name your stuffed animals (ideas: Porky the Pig, Booboo the Bear, Leo the Lion).

Prayer:
Dear God, thank You for making everything beautiful and good for us to enjoy. Thank You for making men and women (boys and girls) to be friends and helpers to each other. Amen.

GOD STOPPED TO REST
GENESIS 2:1-3

And on the seventh day God rested from all his work. *Hebrews 4:4*

_____, do you know what God did after He finished making everything? He stopped for a day to rest. Do you remember all the things He made? He put the moon, sun, and stars in the sky. He made animals. He put fish in the water. He made birds to fly in the air. And then He made a man and a woman to take care of all these things. The Bible calls everything that God made "creation." It was God's special work.

After God finished His work of creation, He stopped and rested. He said, "This is a special day. It is different from all other days. I am happy and pleased with the work I have done. I am going to celebrate and rest today."

Sometimes *we* get tired after we work or play hard. Then we need to rest. God says that is a good thing to do. God is different than we are. God never gets tired, but He does think that it is important to stop working and rest. And He wants us to do that also.

Questions:
1. What did God do after He finished making everything? (He rested for a day.)
2. What does the Bible call God's special work? (creation)

Activities:
1. Talk about different kinds of work. Examples: Dad's work, Mom's work, children's work (playing hard, cleaning room, helping with a younger brother or sister).
2. Draw a picture of examples of different kinds of work (ideas: teacher, plumber, doctor, musician).

Prayer:
Dear God, You think it is good for me to rest after I work or play. Help me obey Mom and Dad when they want me to rest. Thank You. Amen.

GOD MADE ME, TOO!
PSALM 139:1-18; GENESIS 1:27

The Lord formed you while you were still in your mother's body.
Isaiah 44:24

_____, when is your birthday? How old are you? Before you were born (insert age of child) years ago, God knew you and loved you. He is the one who first knew if you would have blue or brown eyes, blond, red or brown hair. He knew what your parents' names would be and if you would have a brother or sister.

God made the sun and moon, trees and flowers, animals and birds. But He also made you. You are very special! God made your mouth and tongue. He knew the first word you would ever say! God made your legs, feet, and toes. He knew when you would take your first step.

God knows everything about you. He knows when you are smiling and when you are crying. The Bible says He even knows when you will sit down. He knows when you get up from a nap (Psalm 139:2). He cares about you. He always knows where you are: at preschool, at church, with the babysitter, at Grandma's house.

God loves you. He always watches over you.

Questions:

1. Who and what did God make? (trees, flowers, sun, moon, animals, and me)

2. What does God know about you? (refer to story above)

3. Who does God love? (me)

Activities:

1. Have your child look into a mirror. Say, "God made me, too!"

2. Attach a photo of your child (or have him draw a picture of himself) to this page. Write the words: GOD MADE _____. Let him write his name in the blank.

Prayer:

Dear God, You made me. You knew about me before I was born. You always know where I am, what I'm doing, and what I'm thinking. I believe that You love me and care about me. Thank You. Amen.

WHO TRICKED ADAM AND EVE?
GENESIS 3:1-7

Eve was tricked by the snake with his evil ways. *2 Corinthians 11:3*

_____, do you like to walk in the park? The trees and flowers are pretty to see, aren't they? A long time ago, God made a beautiful place for Adam and Eve to live. It was like a park. Everything was perfect. The sun shone every day. The fruit on the trees tasted good. Big strong lions played with little furry lambs. God walked and talked with Adam and Eve. They loved living in the Garden of Eden. But one day something happened to change everything.

A snake-like creature came to Eve. He could talk. "Eve, did God tell you not to eat from the trees around here?" he asked.

"Oh, no," said Eve. "God said that we can eat the fruit of any tree, except for one. He said not to touch that fruit, though, or we will die."

Then the creature said, "But, Eve, you won't die! When you eat from this tree, you'll think like God. You'll know everything He knows." The creature was lying to Eve, but she didn't seem to know it. So Eve listened to the lies. She looked at the fruit. It looked pretty good.

"Maybe it will make me smart like God," Eve thought. She reached out and picked the fruit. She took a bite. Then she handed the fruit to her husband, Adam. He took a bite. Eve and Adam looked at each other. Uh oh! They had disobeyed God! That lying creature had tricked them.

Questions:

1. Who lived in the park-like garden? (Adam and Eve)

2. Who lied to Eve? (the snake-like creature)

3. Who disobeyed God? (Adam and Eve)

Activities:

1. Draw a picture of the garden when it was perfect (ideas: animals playing together, sunshine, flowers, trees).

2. Take an imaginary walk in the garden.

Prayer:

Dear God, please help me not to even listen when someone starts to tell lies about You. I want to obey You. Amen.

IT'S NOT MY FAULT!
GENESIS 3:7-19

I have not hidden my sin as other men do. Job 31:33

_____, have you ever tried to hide after you did something naughty? Did you think it would keep you from getting into "trouble"? After Adam and Eve disobeyed God and ate from the special tree, they knew they were wrong.

"Eve, let's hide behind these trees, so God can't find us," said Adam.

At about dinner time, they heard God walking in the garden. "Where are you, Adam?" God called.

"I'm here, God," Adam answered. "I was afraid, so I tried to hide."

"Why were you afraid?" asked God. "Did you eat that fruit I told you not to eat?"

"Yes," said Adam, "But it's not my fault. Eve made me do it."

"Eve," said God, "what have you done?"

"It's not my fault, God! The creature made me do it!"

God was very sad. Adam and Eve had disobeyed Him. "Everything will not always be perfect for you anymore,"God said. "You will have to work hard to get food. Sometimes you may get hurt and cry."

Sadness and hurt came to Adam and Eve when they disobeyed God. When sadness and pain came to the garden, it came to the whole world. Even though Adam and Eve disobeyed, God still loved them. He loves us, too, even when we disobey; even when we are sad. He is happy when we do not try to hide from Him. We can *always* talk to God.

Questions:

1. Why did Adam and Eve hide from God? (They were afraid because they had disobeyed God.)

2. When did sadness and hurt come into the world? (when Adam and Eve disobeyed God)

Activities:

1. Ask your child to make a "sad" face, "afraid" face, "loving" face.

2. Build a "perfectly good" house or building with a set of blocks. Then have your child knock it down to show it's not "perfectly good" anymore (just like the garden after Adam and Eve disobeyed).

Prayer

Dear God, I know You love me all the time. You love me whether I am happy or sad. Even when I disobey, You love and care about me. Thank You. Amen.

BOBBY MAKES A CHOICE
JOSHUA 24:14-16

We will obey the Lord our God. *Jeremiah 42:6*

_____, do you know what it means to "make a choice"? "Making a choice" means that you have to make up your mind what you want to do or say about something. One day last summer, Bobby had to make a choice.

Bobby and his friend, David, were playing ball in the backyard. Bobby threw the ball to David. David swung hard at the ball. "What a hit!" yelled David. He ran fast around the bases while Bobby chased after the ball. But Bobby didn't get the ball in time. David had a homerun!

"Bobby, see that new boy over there?" asked David, after he touched home base. "I think he wants to play with us. But I've seen him play. He can't hit homeruns. Don't ask him to play with us, OK?"

Bobby was quiet. He had a choice to make. Should he do what his friend, David, wanted? Or should he do the right and good thing? He knew that God wanted him to be kind to others, to share with others. This was a hard choice. He didn't want his friend, David, to be mad at him. But Bobby wanted to obey God.

So Bobby said, "David, I'm going to ask that boy to play with us. I don't care if he hits homeruns. And God doesn't either."

Bobby made a good choice. He chose to obey God.

Questions:
1. Who had to "make a choice"? (Bobby)
2. What did Bobby choose? (He chose to obey God and ask the boy to play.)

Activity:
Choose what to eat for breakfast or lunch. Or choose what to wear today.

Prayer:
Dear God, I want to make choices that make You happy. Please help me. Thank You. Amen.

WALKING WITH GOD
GENESIS 5:22-24

Enoch walked with God. *Genesis 5:24*

_____, do you like to take walks? It's fun to walk to the park on a sunny day, isn't it? It's fun to walk in the "fall" leaves and hear the "crackling" sound. It's even fun to put on a coat, hat, mittens, and boots to take a walk in the clean white snow. Every day we walk. We walk down the steps. We walk into the kitchen to eat breakfast. We walk outside to get into the car. Walking gets us where we want to go.

Genesis is the name of the first book in the Bible. In chapter five there is a very short but very special story. The story is about a man named Enoch.

The Bible says that Enoch walked with God. He did not take a short walk with God. He walked with God for 300 years. That is a long time. He and God spent lots of time together.

One day, something very different happened. When Enoch was 365 years old, he disappeared. The Bible says that God took him. God and Enoch enjoyed walking and talking with each other so much. One day when they were walking together, God must have said, "Come, Enoch, come be with me in heaven."

Questions:
1. What is the first book in the Bible? (Genesis)
2. Who walked with God for 300 years? (Enoch)
3. What happened to Enoch when he was 365 years old? (He disappeared. God took him to heaven to be with Him.)

Activities:
1. Show your child where to find Genesis in the Bible.
2. Plan to take a walk with your child.

Prayer:
Dear God, I want to spend time with You. I want to get to know You. Help me to know how to walk (or spend time) with You. Thank You. Amen.

A MAN CALLED NOAH
GENESIS 6:1-13

I have good plans for you. I plan to give you hope. Jeremiah 29:11

_____, do you know what a "population explosion" is? It is when lots of men and women have babies. And then those babies grow up, get married, and have more babies. Then the cities, states, and countries have many people. Lots of people crowd into the houses, schools, churches, and stores. That is a population explosion.

A long time ago there was a population explosion on the earth that God made. God looked from heaven and saw all these people. But He also saw a big problem. That made God very sad. The many people did not love God. They acted like God did not create them. The people were stealing, lying, cheating, and killing all the time.

God said, "I am sad. These people have forgotten me, so I am going to take them off my earth."

But God found one man who loved Him. His name was Noah. Noah believed God, and God was very happy with him. Noah always wanted to please God. So, one day, God said, "Noah, I have a plan for you. Listen carefully and I will tell you my plan."

God has a plan for you and me, too. We can listen carefully to His words in the Bible and learn about His plan.

Questions:

1. What made God sad? (The people lied, cheated, stole, and killed all the time. They had forgotten God.)

2. Who believed and loved God? (Noah)

Activity:

Count the children who live on your street. Then think of *all* the streets with children. Is there a population explosion?

Prayer:

Dear God, You had a plan for Noah. I believe You have a plan for me, too. Please show me about this plan as I listen to Bible stories. Amen.

WHAT DO THE NEIGHBORS THINK?
GENESIS 6:1-18

Work as if you were working for the Lord, not for men.

Colossians 3:23

_____, have you ever ridden on a big boat? Noah and his three sons, Shem, Ham and Japheth, built a *very* b-i-g boat.

God said, "Noah, I know that you want to obey me. I am pleased with you. I have a special plan for you and your family. I want you to build a big boat. You, your wife, and your sons and their wives are going to live on this boat. It is going to rain. Water will cover the ground, but you will be safe inside the boat. The water will cover up the people who do lots of bad things all the time. They have forgotten me. So get ready, Noah! I will tell you how to build this boat."

What God told Noah to do was different from anything that had ever been done before. It had never rained! There probably had never been a boat! Noah's neighbors watched him cut the wood and hammer it together. "What are you doing?" they asked.

"I'm doing what God told me to do. I'm building a boat because it's going to rain and flood the ground," said Noah. "Do you want to help?"

But Noah's neighbors just laughed. "You are crazy for believing God," they said. But they did not stop Noah and his family from building the boat. They believed and obeyed God.

Questions:

1. Who obeyed and believed God even when other people did not? (Noah and his family)

2. What did God ask Noah to do? (build a boat)

Activities:

1. Build a boat with blocks.

2. Draw a picture of Noah's family when they built the boat.

Prayer:

Dear God, Noah believed You. He worked hard on the boat even when his neighbors did not believe him. Help me to obey You and work hard even when my friends do not. Thank You. Amen.

THE FLOATING ZOO
GENESIS 6:14-22

Lord, you have made many things. With your
wisdom you made them all. *Psalm 104:24*

_____, do you like
to visit the animals at the zoo? There are
lots of different kinds of animals, aren't
there? Elephants, giraffes, monkeys,
chickens, bears, and deer are some of the
animals you see at the zoo. Noah spent
time with all these animals. He built a big
boat. He made it with lots of rooms. He
brought animals, birds, and crawling
things into the boat with him. "Bring a
mommy and a daddy animal of every
kind," said God. "Take enough food to feed your family and the
animals."

God called the large boat, Noah's ark. The ark was so-o-o big. It
was longer than four houses put beside each other. It was taller than
three houses stacked on top of each other. The ark held hundreds of
animals in all the rooms.

Think of all the noise that hundreds of animals and birds made. The
cows went "moo," the cats went "meow." The monkeys chattered,
and the lions roared. God made them all live together peacefully in
Noah's ark. It was a big floating zoo.

Questions:
1. How big was Noah's ark? (longer than four houses and taller
than three houses stacked on top of each other)
2. What did Noah bring with him into the ark? (a mommy and a
daddy of every kind of animal)

Activities:
1. Name animals starting with the letters of the alphabet (ideas: A =
anteater; B = bear; C = cow; D = donkey).
2. Make animal sounds for some of the animals you named.

Prayer:
Dear God, You made every animal, bird, and crawling thing. You
made man. Thank You for saving some of all that you made in the
ark, the floating zoo. Amen.

NOAH AND THE RAIN
GENESIS 7:17—8:5

These refused to obey God long ago in the time of Noah.
Only a few people—eight in all—were saved.

1 Peter 3:20

Have you ever watched the rain hit hard against a window? Have you seen lightning across the sky? Have you heard loud thunder crack between the clouds?

_____, what is the longest time you have seen it rain? Maybe for a day (maybe two). But what if it rained without stopping for 40 days and 40 nights? That would be a lot of rain, wouldn't it?

Noah and his family saw a lot of rain. It rained all the time for 40 days. But Noah, his family, and the animals stayed dry inside the special boat.

There have been many floods, but none like this one. This flood was over the entire earth. The water was so deep that it covered the highest mountain tops. The flood waters covered all the bad people who forgot to listen to and obey God. It covered the grass and plants and trees. But everyone and everything in the boat was saved. After 40 days, it stopped raining.

But it took time for the water to start to go away. After seven months, the floating boat stopped on top of a mountain. The mountain was called Ararat. Noah and his family had been on the boat for a long time.

But God did not forget Noah and his family. God never forgets his children.

Questions:
1. How long did it rain? (40 days and 40 nights)
2. When did the ark stop floating? (after seven months)
3. On what mountain did the ark stop? (Mount Ararat)

Activities:
1. Draw a picture of rain and lightning and the clouds.
2. Sing "Row, Row, Row Your Boat."

Prayer:
Dear God, I'm sure Noah and his family sometimes wondered if the water would ever go away. But You did not forget them. You will not forget me, either. Thank You. Amen.

SEE THE RAINBOW?
GENESIS 8:16-22; GENESIS 9:8-17

That rainbow is a sign. *Genesis 9:17*

_____, have you ever seen a rainbow in the sky? It has pretty colors, doesn't it? Noah saw the very first colorful rainbow. Here is the story about that first rainbow.

Noah and his family had been in the boat for a long time. One day Noah said, "Let's open a window and send out a bird to see if it can find any dry land."

But the bird just kept flying around. So Noah tried again. But that bird came back without finding a dry place to build a nest. After waiting seven more days, Noah tried again. This time the bird flew back through the window with a leaf in its beak. One week later, Noah sent the bird out the window again. This time the bird found a dry place to build a nest. It never came back to the boat.

Then God said, "It's time now, Noah. The ground is dry. You can all leave the boat."

Noah and his family were so happy. They hugged each other. They were thankful. Noah prayed to God. God was pleased with Noah's thankful prayer.

God said, "I will not let water cover the whole earth again. There will never be another flood like this. I am putting a pretty rainbow of colors into the sky. Each time I see the rainbow, I will remember my promise."

Questions:
1. What did Noah send out the window? (a bird)
2. Did Noah thank God for keeping them safe? (Yes. He prayed a thankful prayer to God.)
3. Why did God send a rainbow? (as a promise that there will never be another flood like this one)

Activities:
1. Have your child color the rainbow on the facing page. Name the colors.
2. Look together for a rainbow the next time it rains.

Prayer:
Dear God, thank You for taking care of Noah and his family. Thank You for the pretty rainbow You put in the sky. Thank You for Your promise. Amen.

SLIDING DOWN RAINBOWS
GENESIS 9:13-17

I am putting my rainbow in the clouds. *Genesis 9:13*

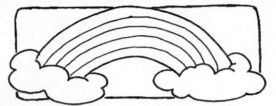

"Come here, Jody," called her big sister, Mandy. "Hurry, I want to show you something." She pulled the curtain back and looked out the kitchen window.

Jody ran across the room to stand beside Mandy. "It's a rainbow!" she said excitedly. "I love rainbows! God is telling me He loves me. He'll never have a big bad flood again."

"Blue, green, yellow, pink, purple. Look at all the pretty colors," said eight-year-old Mandy. "I'd like to have a dress with all those beautiful colors."

"You know what, Mandy? When I get to heaven, I want to slide down rainbows. Wouldn't that be fun?"

_____, God made the colorful rainbow to show us that He thinks about us, and that He loves us and cares about us. God is a good God. I think God is happy when we look at his pretty rainbow and smile.

Questions:
   1. Who called to Jody? (her big sister, Mandy)
   2. What did they see out the window? (a rainbow)
   3. Who wanted to slide down rainbows? (Jody)
   4. Who made the rainbow? (God)

Activities:
   1. Name colors that you may find in a rainbow. (violet, indigo, blue, green, yellow, orange, red)
   2. If weather permits, go to the park and slide down the slide. Pretend it is a rainbow.

Prayer:
   Dear God, I smile when I see Your rainbow in the sky. You make such pretty things. Someday I will be with You in heaven. That will be fun. Amen.

WHERE ARE YOU GOING, ABRAM?
GENESIS 12:1-6

Abraham believed God. *Romans 4:3*

_____, have you ever moved to a new house, away from your friends? Or started to go to a different school or church? Did you sometimes feel lonely? Did things seem different to you?

Maybe Abram felt that same way. One day, God came to Abram and said, "Leave your home and your friends. I will tell you where to move. I'm going to make you great. From your children will come a very big nation. I promise I will always take care of you."

So Abram did just what God told him to do. Abram did not know where he was going, but he believed God would take care of him.

Abram was 75 years old when he heard God tell him to move. He took his wife, Sarai, his brother's son, Lot, and all of his animals and servants. Cows, sheep, and people with all their clothes and food moved like a parade down the road. When they arrived in Canaan, God again came to Abram.

"Look at this land," God said. "I promise you that I will give this land to your children, grandchildren, and great-grandchildren, and even their children." Abraham believed God. He built a special place called an altar, and there he prayed to God.

Questions:

1. Who went with Abram when God told him to move? (his wife, Sarai; his brother's son, Lot; servants; and animals)

2. What did God promise Abram? (to give land to his children)

Activities:

1. Gather your stuffed animals and toys into a parade. Pretend to travel like Abram did.

2. Draw a picture of Abram and his parade.

Prayer:

Dear God, Abram obeyed You even when he didn't understand. Maybe he felt lonely, but he believed You would take care of him. I want to obey and believe You also. Amen.

ABRAM SHARES
GENESIS 13:5-11

Be happy to give and ready to share. *1 Timothy 6:18*

Lot lived with his uncle, Abram, for many years. Lot had cows, sheep, and servants of his own. His farm grew to be very big. And Abram's farm grew to be very big. The cows had lots of babies called calves. The sheep had babies called lambs. The servants had babies, too.

But there were so many animals and people that there was not room on the land for everyone. What could they do? Soon they would not have enough grass for all the animals to eat. Already the shepherds were fighting about the land. This made Abram sad. He said, "Lot, let's stop the fighting between our shepherds and servants. We will have to divide up. You and your animals and people go one way. I will go another way. You decide which way you want to go."

So Lot looked out over the land. He saw the green grass by the Jordan River. It was beautiful country. He thought about his sheep and cows. The grass looked very juicy for his animals to eat. He knew it was the best land.

So he said, "I'll take the land by the river."

Lot acted selfishly. He wanted all the best land for himself. He didn't really care about his uncle, Abram. But Abram shared.

_____, do you care about your family and friends enough to share (unselfishly) with them?

Questions:
1. Why did the servant and shepherds fight? (because there was not enough room on the land for everyone)
2. Who acted selfishly and chose the best land for himself? (Lot)

Activities:
1. Name animals and their young (see examples in the story).
2. Put a star on this page every time your child shares tomorrow.

Prayer:
Dear God, I want to be a sharing boy (girl) like Abram was. Please help me to remember to share. Thank You. Amen.

SELFISH LOT IS SAD
GENESIS 13:11-13; 2 PETER 2:7, 8

When you do things, do not let selfishness be your guide.
Philippians 2:3

_____, have you ever wanted the biggest cupcake for yourself? Or have you ever cried because you wanted Mommy to stop feeding baby sister to play with you right now?

Sometimes we want all the good things just for us and no one else. That is being selfish. Lot was selfish. He wanted all the juicy grass for his own sheep and cows. He didn't care about Uncle Abram and his animals. So he made up his mind to move to a place by the water. But Lot's selfish decision was not a smart one. It really was not good for him or his family.

The beautiful land by the water was near the city of Sodom. Many bad people lived in Sodom. Lot's neighbors and friends did not love God. Lot wanted to love and pray to God, but it was very hard to do in wicked Sodom.

Lot made a selfish decision, because he thought it would be good for his family and animals. But it was a sad choice. When we make up our mind to be selfish it is a sad choice for us, too.

Questions:

1. How did Lot act selfishly? (He took all the best land for his family and his animals.)

2. What was the name of the town where Lot and his family lived? (Sodom)

3. Did the people in Sodom love God? (no)

4. Did Lot make a good decision? (no)

Activity:

Draw a picture of Lot's sheep eating the juicy grass. Draw sad faces on Lot and his children.

Prayer:

Dear God, help me to share. I don't want to be selfish like Lot. Amen.

WHERE ARE THE COOKIES?
PROVERBS 3:1-7; GENESIS 12:18-20; 13:10-13

Don't ever stop being kind and truthful. *Proverbs 3:3*

Nancy stopped swinging. "I have an idea," she said to her little brother, Michael. "Let's ask Mom if we can take some of the cookies she's baking to Bobby." Bobby lived next door and he had a broken leg. Every day he sat by the window watching Nancy and Michael in the yard. He looked sad. He missed playing outside with his friends.

"OK," said four-year-old Michael. "But I want some cookies, too."

"Maybe Mom will let us have one. I'll go see." Nancy ran inside.

"Michael, Mom said yes," yelled Nancy through the screen door.

Michael hurried into the kitchen. "I'm hungry," he thought. "I won't get many cookies if we share them *all* with Bobby. I better

make sure I get enough for me. So he picked up ten extra cookies when Mom and Nancy weren't looking. He ran to his room to hide them under his bed.

After wrapping the cookies, they ran to Bobby's house. Bobby clapped when his friends came to the door. "I like cookies," he said.

After dinner Mom went to the cookie jar. It was empty! "Where are the cookies?" she asked.

"I don't know," said Nancy.

"I didn't have any," said Dad. "Did you, Michael?"

Michael lied. "No, and I don't know where they are." Then Michael began to cry. "I hid the cookies. I'm sorry. Do you still love me?"

"Yes, Michael," said Dad. "What you did was wrong, but God always loves you, and so do we."

Questions:
1. Who took cookies to Bobby? (Michael and Nancy)
2. Does God still love Michael even though he lied? (yes)

Activity:
Make (or buy) cookies together. Then, share with a friend.

Prayer:
Dear God, I don't want to be selfish or lie. Help me to remember to share and tell the truth. Thank You for always loving me. Amen.

WHAT IS FAITH?
GENESIS 15:1-6

Abraham believed God, and God
accepted Abraham's faith. *Galatians 3:6*

God promised Abram that he would have lots of grandchildren. But Abram and his wife, Sarai, did not have any babies.

"I don't know how this is going to work," said Abram. "How can I have lots of grandchildren when I don't even have a son?" Abram was very sad.

But God said, "Abram, don't worry. I will keep my promise. I know you don't have a baby right now, but I promise you that someday you will have a baby boy."

Then Abram believed that what God was telling him was the truth. "God ALWAYS tells the truth," thought Abram. "And God has always taken care of me and my family. I know God will keep His promise."

_____, when you believe something is true, it means that you have "faith." Abram had faith. He had faith in God. It made God very happy when Abram believed Him. God likes it when we have "faith" in what He says, too.

Questions:

1. Who promised Abram that one day he would have a baby boy? (God)

2. Did Abram believe God's words? (yes)

3. What does it mean to have "faith"? (Having faith means believing something is true.)

Activities:

1. Turn on the light switch. You believed—you had "faith"—that the light would come on, and it did.

2. Write your name at the bottom of this page, then write "has faith" after your name.

Prayer:

Dear God, I know that You *always* tell the truth. I believe You. I have "faith" in You. Amen.

AMY HELPS DANNY BY PRAYING
GENESIS 19:29

And you can help us with your prayers. *2 Corinthians 1:11*

Danny stood by the door. "Where's my mom?" he cried. "She's never coming back! I want my mom!"

"Don't cry, Danny," said his friend Amy. "Your mom will be back. Come play with us."

"No," cried Danny. "She's not coming back! I don't wanna play!"

Amy looked sad. She knew Danny's mom was coming back. But Danny just would not believe it. Then Amy had an idea.

"Miss Judy," she said to her teacher, "can we pray for Danny? Let's pray that he'll believe his mom is coming back."

"That's a good idea, Amy," said Miss Judy. "Let's pray that he'll stop crying and wait quietly for his mother." So Amy and Miss Judy prayed for Danny while the other children and Miss Susan read a story.

"Listen, Miss Judy," said Amy, "Danny has stopped crying!"

Danny peeked around the corner. "It looks like the other kids are having fun," he thought. "Maybe I can, too." So Danny sat down beside Amy. They listened to stories, sang, colored, and played together. After awhile there was a knock on the door. The teacher walked over to open it. There stood Danny's mom.

"Mom, I knew you'd come," Danny said smiling. "I waited for you."

Amy and Miss Judy looked at each other. They were happy that `God answered their prayer for Danny.

Questions:
1. Who prayed for Danny? (Miss Judy and Amy)
2. Did God answer their prayer? (yes)

Activity:
Decide who to pray for today and how to pray for them (examples: Help Chuckie not to cry at the babysitter's; or help Aunt Jane to get a new job). Fill in the blanks below.

Prayer:
Dear God, please help _____ to _____. Thank You. Amen.

30

NEW NAMES FOR ABRAM AND SARAI
GENESIS 17:1-8, 15, 16

And Abraham was called "God's friend."
James 2:23

_____, when Abram was 99 years old, God changed his name. "I am going to call you Abraham from now on," said God. "I am doing this because you are going to be the grandfather of many people. Kings will come from you. Remember, Abraham, that I will be your God. I will be the one to take care of you."

Abraham listened to what God told him. Abraham and God were very special friends.

"I am going to change your wife's name, also," God said, "It will sound the same, but it will be spelled differently. Her new name is Sarah spelled S-a-r-a-h. This is a special day for her, because I am promising her that next year at this time she will have a baby boy. Abraham, you and Sarah will become Great-grandpa and Great-grandma to many people."

Today, the people who live in Israel are relatives of Abraham and Sarah. These people are called Jews. Sometimes they are called Israelites or Israelis.

Questions:
1. How old was Abram when God changed his name? (He was 99 years old.)
2. What was Abram's new name? (Abraham)
3. What was Sarai's new name? (Sarah, spelled with an "h")
4. Who was God's special friend? (Abraham)

Activities:
1. Count to 99.
2. Say your whole name.

Prayer:
Dear God, You were Abraham and Sarah's God, and You are my God, too. You were with them, and You are with me, also. Thank You. Amen.

GOD CAN DO ANYTHING
GENESIS 18:1-15

You know that nothing is
impossible for me. *Jeremiah 32:27*

_____, do you see the picture of Abraham? Abraham lived in a home that looked like a very big tent. Three men came to visit him at his tent one day. Abraham was kind to them. He gave them water to drink. Abraham invited the three men to eat dinner at his tent-house.

"Where is Sarah, your wife?" asked the men.

"She's inside the tent," answered Abraham.

Abraham had never seen these three men before. They gave Abraham a special message from God. "Your wife will have a baby boy by this time next year," they said.

Sarah was listening behind the tent door. She heard what these men said and laughed. "These men must be joking," she thought. "I am too old to have a baby now." Sarah did not know that these three men were really from God.

"Doesn't Sarah believe us?" they asked. "Remember that nothing is too hard for God. He has promised to give you a baby boy, and He will do it."

Then the three men from God left Abraham and Sarah's tent-house. They gave Abraham and Sarah very special words of hope—next year they would have a baby!

Questions;
1. What was Abraham's house like? (a big tent)
2. Who visited Abraham? (three men)
3. Where did these three men come from? (They came from God.)
4. What did they tell Abraham? (Sarah will have a baby boy by next year.)
5. What did Sarah do when she heard this news? (She laughed.)

Activities:
1. Make a "pretend" tent. Spread a large sheet or blanket over two chairs.
2. Play inside the tent.

Prayer:
Dear God, You are the God of every person. I know that nothing is too hard for You. Amen.

A BABY BOY IS BORN!
GENESIS 21:1-7

You are God's children because of
his promise, as Isaac was then. *Galatians 4:28*

_____, what do you
do when you are happy? Do you laugh? People sometimes laugh when they are very happy.

Sarah was very happy. She said, "God has made me laugh." What happened to make her so glad?

Sarah had wanted a baby for a long time. God promised that He would give a baby son to Sarah and her husband, Abraham. And He did. Everything happened just the way God said it would. Sarah had a baby boy! Sarah and Abraham named him Isaac. The name "Isaac" means "laughing."

"Everyone will be so happy to hear about our baby. They will laugh," said Sarah. "I was too old to have a baby, but God made it happen."

God made a promise to Abraham. Then he promised Sarah, too. He promised them that they would have a baby boy. God's promises always come true.

Questions:

1. Why was Sarah so happy? (God had kept His promise and given her a baby.)

2. What did Abraham and Sarah name the baby? (Isaac)

3. What does the name "Isaac" mean? (laughing)

Activity:

1. Smile at your child. Have your child smile back at you. Now laugh together.

2. Tell your child what his(her) name means. Share the reason why you chose that name.

Prayer:

Dear God, Sarah was happy that You kept Your promise to her when You gave her baby Isaac. I am happy that You keep Your promises to me, too. Amen.

A SERVANT'S PRAYER
GENESIS 24:1-27

I asked the Lord for help, and he answered me. Psalm 34:4

_____, someday when you are older, you may get married. It's important to ask God for help in choosing whom to marry. Abraham wanted his son, Isaac, to marry a girl who loved God. He asked God for help in finding a wife for Isaac. Abraham had a plan. . . .

Abraham asked his favorite servant to go to a different city to look for a wife for Isaac. Abraham knew this man would do a good job.

Abraham's servant took animals and gifts for the lady. He traveled far. Finally he rested beside a well of water. His animals were thirsty, and so was he. While he sat by the well, he prayed to God.

"Please help me find a wife for Isaac," he prayed. "Would You please have a nice girl come here to the well and get a drink for me and my animals. Then I will know that You've helped me."

Before the servant finished praying, a girl walked up to the well. She was very pretty. She got water to put in her jug. When the servant asked for a drink, she was very kind. She gave drinks to the servant and his animals. The servant watched her closely. She seemed to be the kind of girl he was looking for. God was answering the servant's prayer.

The servant bowed his head. "Lord, God, You are helping me," he prayed. "Thank You for being so kind." The servant prayed to God when he needed help. We, too, can pray to God when we need help.

Questions:
1. What kind of girl did Abraham want Isaac to marry? (a girl who loved God)
2. Did the servant pray for help in finding a wife for Isaac? (yes)

Activity:
Pretend to get water from the well. Then pretend to water the animals (using stuffed animal as props if available).

Prayer:
Dear God, I need help tomorrow when I _____. Please help me. I will watch for Your answer. Amen.

MEETING REBEKAH'S FAMILY
GENESIS 24:28-52

And when you pray, always give thanks.
Philippians 4:6

_____, do you have a friend named Rebecca? It's a nice name, isn't it? Rebekah was the name of the kind girl who gave Abraham's servant a drink of water. After Rebekah gave the servant and his animals a drink, she ran home. She told her family about the man at the well.

"He gave me a ring and two bracelets," she said. "He is very kind. He prayed to our God. And he wants to come stay all night at our house."

So Rebekah's brother, Laban, went out to meet the servant-man. "Come on in to the house," he said. "You're probably hungry. Here's some food for you to eat." But the man did not eat.

"First I want to tell you why I'm here," the servant said. "Abraham, who is part of your family, told me to come. Abraham wants a wife for his son, Isaac. He wants Isaac to marry a girl who loves God. So I came here because your family loves and worships God. I asked God to help me find a wife when I was at the well. Then He sent Rebekah. God had answered my prayer. It was then that I bowed my head to thank God."

Laban and Rebekah's father listened to the servant-man's story. Then they said, "We believe you. God is surely the one who answered your prayer. Rebekah can go to marry Isaac."

Then the servant-man closed his eyes to thank God. We can thank God for His answers to our prayers, too.

Questions:
1. Who went to meet Rebekah's family? (Abraham's servant)
2. Did Rebekah's father say that she could marry Isaac? (yes)

Activities:
1. Make a ring or bracelet out of paper and tape.
2. Parents: Abraham's servant talked to Rebekah's brother, Laban, and her father, Bethuel. Rebekah's grandfather, Nahor, was Abraham's brother. If possible, compare the relationship to one of your child's relatives.

Prayer:
Dear God, thank You for answering my prayers (be specific). Amen.

LET'S GET MARRIED!
GENESIS 24:54-67

Anyone who comes to God must believe that he is real.

Hebrews 11:6

Abraham's servant-man had a good night's sleep at the home of Rebekah. In the morning he packed his things. "I'm leaving to go back to Abraham this morning. Is Rebekah ready to go?"

Rebekah's mother and brother said, "Please wait ten days. We'll miss Rebekah so much. We want a longer time to say good-bye."

The servant said, "God has answered my prayer. Please don't make me wait." So they asked Rebekah what she wanted to do.

"I'm ready to go meet Isaac now," she said. Even through Rebekah did not know where she was going, she knew that God would take care of her on this long trip. So she packed up and left.

Isaac was walking in the field when the servant-man got home with Rebekah. The servant told Isaac how he met Rebekah. He told Isaac how God answered his prayer. Isaac was very happy. "Let's get married," he said. He loved Rebekah right from the start.

God cared about each person in this story. He answered the servant's prayer. He gave Isaac a loving wife. And He helped Rebekah when she left her family. They all believed that God would take care of them.

_____, God cares about you, too. He will always take care of you.

Questions:

1. Who left her family to go with the servant? (Rebekah)
2. Who was walking in the field? (Isaac)
3. Who got married? (Isaac and Rebekah)

Activity:

Pretend to be in a wedding (ideas: put sheet on head for veil, walk down the aisle, put ring on finger).

Prayer:

Dear God, the servant, Isaac, and Rebekah believed You would help them. I believe that You will help me, too. Amen.

TWINS
GENESIS 25:19-26

God can do much, much more than anything
we can ask or think of. *Ephesians 3:20*

_____, have you ever played with twins? Twins
are two children born to the same parents on the same day.

One day God said, "Rebekah, you are going to have twins."

This was a surprise to Rebekah. Rebekah prayed to God about the
two babies that were growing inside of her.

God said, "One twin will be a leader to the other twin. The first one
will not be the leader. The second one to be born will be stronger than
the first one." This was very different news. Always before, the first
boy born to a mom and dad was the leader. God was saying something very different.

"I think it's time for me to have my twins," said Rebekah to her

husband, Isaac, one day. They named
the first baby boy, Esau. He was born
with a lot of hair. The second boy was
named Jacob. Although Jacob and Esau
were twins, they did not look alike or
act alike. These twins were very different.

Isaac had prayed for a baby. God answered his prayer. In fact, God answered his prayer more than Isaac even
thought about. Isaac had prayed for one
baby. Now he had two babies. Sometimes God answers our prayers
more than we can even think about.

Questions:
1. Who was going to have twins? (Rebekah)
2. Which twin would be the leader? (Jacob, the second one born)
3. Who prayed that Rebekah would have a baby? (Isaac)

Activity:
Pretend to hold two babies at the same time (maybe hold two
dolls). Try to feed them both at the same time.

Prayer:
Dear God, sometimes You answer our prayers much better than we
can even think about. Thank You. Amen.

ESAU AND THE BOWL OF SOUP
GENESIS 25:29-34

Be careful that no person is like Esau and never thinks about God.
Hebrews 12:16

_____, do you remember the twin baby boys named Esau and Jacob? They grew up to be young men. They were twins, but they were not alike. Esau did not really care about God, but Jacob believed God's promises. Here is a story about what happened to them one day.

Esau was a hunter. One time after hunting all day, Esau came home very tired and hungry. As he walked in the door, he smelled Jacob's soup cooking on the stove.

"I am starving," said Esau. "Give me some of your soup."

"I will give you some soup if you give me your part of Dad's money and blessing-gifts," said Jacob.

"Well, I'm so hungry, it doesn't matter to me," said Esau. "I guess you can have the money and gifts that Dad was going to give me." So Esau made a promise to Jacob. Then he sat down and ate the soup.

Esau made a bad decision. He gave away the money his father had saved for him. He didn't care about planning for tomorrow. He didn't care about his own children and how the money and blessings would help them. He only cared about what he wanted right now—his soup.

Esau did not care about God. The blessing-gifts were God's idea, but Esau did not care. He cared about his hungry stomach more than he cared about anything.

Questions:
1. Who gave away his part of his father's money and gifts? (Esau)
2. Did Esau care about God? (no)

Activities:
1. Name different kinds of soup that you like to eat.
2. Pretend to eat your favorite soup together.

Prayer:
Dear God, I don't want to be like Esau. I care about You. Help me make good decisions. Amen.

A MIXED-UP FAMILY
GENESIS 27:1-45

Don't use your mouth to tell lies. *Proverbs 4:24*

The twin brothers Esau and Jacob were very different. Esau liked to be outside. He was a farmer and a hunter. Jacob liked to stay inside. He cooked and helped his mother around the house.

One day Isaac said to his son Esau, "I'm getting old. I can't see very well. I think I'm going to die soon. Let me give you my special blessing-gifts before I die." He said it so Rebekah and Jacob would not hear him. He was trying to hide from them.

But Rebekah, the twins' mother, heard Isaac. She did not like what she heard. "No," she thought, "Jacob is the one who should get the blessing-gifts." So she thought up a "sneaky" plan. She told Jacob to dress up like Esau.

"Let's trick your father," she said. "He can't see very well anyway. If you dress up like Esau, he'll give *you* the blessing-gifts."

So Jacob dressed in Esau's clothes. Then he smelled and felt like his brother Esau. Father Isaac was fooled. He gave Jacob the blessing-gifts.

When Father Isaac found out what had happened, he was sad. His body shook. Esau was mad at Jacob. Jacob had to move away to get away from Esau. And Isaac was sad and alone. Rebekah was afraid because she had lied. Now she was sad because Jacob moved away. The whole family was mixed up. When mothers and fathers and brothers lie to each other, it brings trouble.

_____, God wants us to always tell the truth.

Questions:
1. Who tried to trick Isaac? (Rebekah and Jacob)
2. Does lying bring trouble? (yes)

Activity:
Play dress up. Put on someone else's clothes and pretend to be that person.

Prayer:
Dear God, please help me to use my mouth to tell the truth. Amen.

THE LOST LETTER
GENESIS 27:1-45

Don't ever say things that are not true. *Proverbs 4:24*

"Bradley, please run out to the mailbox and get the mail," said Mom. "I am expecting a very important letter."

"OK, Mom," said Bradley. "I'll be right back." He went to the mailbox. He stood on his tip toes and reached in. There were four letters. On the way back to the house, he saw his friend, Craig, throwing a ball into the air.

"Come on over and play catch," Craig yelled. So Bradley laid the letters on a rock and ran to play ball.

Later, Bradley's mom called him to come home for dinner. Then he remembered the letters. He ran to the rock. The letters were gone! He looked all over. But he couldn't find them. When his mom asked about the mail, he lied. He said, "There was no mail today, Mom."

Two days went by. It was dinner time again. The phone rang. Bradley heard his mom say, "I'm sorry, Grandma, we didn't get your letter. But we'll be right down to get you." Mom slowly hung up the phone. "Let's go get Grandma. She's waiting at the bus station. I don't understand what happened. She says she sent us a letter telling us when to pick her up."

Bradley remembered the lost letters. Tears filled his eyes. "Mom, I'm sorry. I lied about the mail the other day. I lost Grandma's letter."

Bradley was truly sorry. Grandma, Mom, and the whole family forgave him. But Bradley remembered the story about Esau, Jacob, Rebekah, and Isaac. Lying always causes trouble.

_____, you and I can remember that it's best to tell the truth, even when it's hard to do.

Questions:
1. Who lost the letters? (Bradley)
2. Did he lie to his mom? (yes)

Activity:
Plan to write a letter or draw a picture for Grandma. Mail it.

Prayer:
Dear God, help me to tell the truth even when it's hard to do. Amen.

WHAT A DREAM!
GENESIS 28:1-22

Then Jacob made a promise. *Genesis 28:20*

After Jacob left his family, he went to find a wife. He went alone. It was a long trip.

After traveling for awhile, Jacob got very tired. Night time came, and he stopped to rest. He used a rock for a pillow. It wasn't very comfortable. But soon he fell asleep.

Jacob dreamed that a ladder was going from the ground up to heaven. Angels climbed up and down the ladder. God stood at the top. It was a very different dream.

God helped Jacob understand the dream. "I am with you," God said. "I will help you everywhere you go. I promise to give you the land you're sleeping on. It will belong to your children and to their children. I will do everything that I have promised."

Then Jacob woke up. "What a dream!" he thought. "But I know God talked to me. How special that is! I am going to name this place Bethel." Bethel means "house of God."

God made a promise to Jacob. And Jacob made a promise to God. Jacob said, "God has promised to keep me safe on my trip and give me food to eat and clothes to wear. I will worship Him. I will also give Him back one tenth of all He's given me."

_____, Jacob decided to worship and love and pray to God. He also promised to give God part of his wealth. We call that an offering. We can decide to do that, too.

Questions:
1. Who went to find a wife? (Jacob)
2. What did Jacob use as a pillow as he slept under the stars? (a rock)
3. Who talked to Jacob in the dream? (God)
4. Did Jacob promise to worship God? (yes)

Activity:
Put something hard (like a book or a box) under your head for a pillow. Talk about how it feels.

Prayer:
Dear God, I know that You are with me. I promise to love, worship, and pray to You. Amen.

JACOB LOVES RACHEL
GENESIS 29:1-20

Even much water cannot put out the flame of love.
Floods cannot drown love. *Song of Solomon 8:7*

_____, when you and your family go on a long trip, do you walk? No! You go in a car, bus, or plane, don't you? But when Jacob was on his long trip to find a wife, he did not have a car, bus, or plane. He walked or rode on a camel.

This was a hard way to travel. Jacob became tired. He stopped by a well to rest. Soon a pretty young lady brought her sheep to the well to get a drink. Her name was Rachel. She was from Jacob's mother's family. This made Jacob so happy. He hugged Rachel and cried happy tears! Rachel ran home to tell her family.

As soon as Rachel's dad heard the news, he came out to meet Jacob. "Come to my house. You are my family," said Rachel's father, Laban.

Jacob stayed and helped Laban for a month. Then Laban said, "Jacob, how should I pay you for working for me?"

"Please let me marry your daughter, Rachel. I will work for you for seven years, if you will let me marry her," answered Jacob.

Now seven years is a long time, but Jacob loved Rachel so much that it seemed a short time to him. Nothing, not hard work or many waiting years, could keep Jacob from loving Rachel. He loved Rachel, and he waited for her to be his wife. Even the Bible says that nothing can take away true love.

Questions:
1. Why was Jacob happy to see Rachel and Laban? (They were from his mother's family.)
2. Who loved Rachel? (Jacob)

Activity:
Count to seven. Count to the number of years old you are.

Prayer:
Dear God, thank You for creating us so that we can love. Loving is very special. Amen.

LABAN TRICKED JACOB
GENESIS 29:21-30

Do what is right and fair.
Proverbs 21:3

_____, who did Jacob love and want to marry? Yes, he wanted to marry Rachel. Rachel's father promised Jacob that he could marry Rachel if he worked with him and took care of his sheep for seven years.

Jacob worked hard. Each year he knew he was closer to being Rachel's husband. Each year he got more excited.

Finally, the seven years were over. Jacob came to Laban and said, "It's time for me to marry Rachel now."

So Laban planned a big wedding party. But Laban did a mean thing to Jacob. Laban tricked Jacob. A long time ago, brides wore heavy veils over their faces. In the morning after the wedding, Jacob lifted up the heavy veil. What a surprise! He saw a different lady. It was not his lovely Rachel. Jacob had married Rachel's older sister, Leah. Now what could Jacob do? He loved Rachel, not Leah.

Jacob went to Laban. "Why did you trick me?" he said. "I worked so hard for you for seven long years."

Laban said, "I gave you Leah because she is the oldest daughter. You can have Rachel now for your wife, too. But you have to work another seven years." Laban was not fair with Jacob. He lied to Jacob. But Jacob loved Rachel, so he said that he would work for another seven years.

God says it is important to be fair. He does not like it when we lie or trick people like Laban did.

Questions:
1. Who worked seven years for Laban so that he could marry Rachel? (Jacob)
2. Who tricked Jacob? (Laban, Rachel's father)
3. Did Jacob have to work seven more years for Rachel? (yes)
Activity:
Add seven blocks or toys to seven more blocks or toys. How many years did Jacob have to work? (fourteen)
Prayer:
Dear God, help me always to be fair and tell the truth. I know this is important to You. Amen.

ANGELS WATCHING OVER US
GENESIS 31:3, 43-55; 32:1

He has put his angels in charge of you.
They will watch over you wherever you go. *Psalm 91:11*

"Jacob, it's time to leave Laban's house. Take your family and go back to your father's city," said God. "And don't worry, because I will be with you."

While Jacob lived with his father-in-law, Laban, he had eleven sons and one daughter. He also had lots of animals. At first Laban was mad that Jacob was leaving with his daughters, grandchildren, and many animals. But Laban and Jacob talked together.

Laban said, "Let the Lord watch over us while we are apart from each other." He kissed his grandchildren and daughters good-bye.

Then Jacob, Leah, Rachel, and the children left with all their animals and belongings.

While Jacob was on the road something very different happened! God's angels met him! When Jacob saw all the angels, he said, "God is here with me."

_____, God sends His angels to help us and keep us safe. He did that for Jacob. He will do it for us, too. Jacob saw the angels, but usually they are invisible. "Invisible" means that we cannot see something with our eyes. God's angels are like invisible babysitters. They watch over us.

Questions:
1. Who did Jacob meet on the road? (God's angels)
2. Do God's angels help keep us safe? (yes)

Activities:
1. Count to 12. That is the number of children the Bible tells us Jacob had while he lived with Laban.
2. Point to the angel.

Prayer:
Dear God, thank You that your angels watch over me everywhere I go. Amen.

FRIENDS AGAIN
GENESIS 33:1-11

I asked the Lord for help. He saved me from all that I feared.

Psalm 34:4

As Jacob traveled back to his father's city, he was thinking about his twin brother, Esau. Jacob was afraid that Esau might come and hurt him. _____, do you know why Jacob was afraid of Esau?

Twenty years before, Jacob lied to Esau. He stole something from Esau that was very important. Esau was so mad that he wanted to kill Jacob. This was the reason Jacob was afraid of his brother.

God knew Jacob was afraid. God came to Jacob one night. After that meeting with God, Jacob was changed. God even gave Jacob another name—Israel. Jacob decided to make God the most special person in his life. Jacob knew that God would help him not to be so afraid.

"I am truly sorry I lied and cheated my brother, Esau," thought Jacob. "With God's help I am ready to see him again." Jacob did not know what Esau would do. But when Esau saw his twin brother, Jacob, he ran to meet him. They hugged and kissed each other. They cried happy tears.

God helped Jacob and Esau to love and forgive each other. They became friends again. God is bigger and stronger than whoever or whatever we are afraid of.

Questions:

1. Who met with God and was changed? (Jacob)

2. Who helped twin brothers, Jacob and Esau, become friends again? (God)

Activities:

1. Count to 20.

2. Hug each other.

Prayer:

Dear God, Jacob was afraid of Esau, but You helped him. Would You please help me, too? Thank You. Amen.

"I'M SORRY"
GENESIS 33:1-11

Being sorry in the way God wants
makes a person change his heart and life. *2 Corinthians 7:10*

Allison, Carol, and Shannon were friends. They lived on the same street. They liked to play together. One morning they played "store" at Allison's house.

After awhile, Allison had an idea. "Mom, can we play with real money today?" she asked. So Mom took 75 cents out of her purse and said, "Have fun, but be very careful not to lose any of these coins."

The three girls had a good time going up and down the aisles of the "store." They "bought" fruit and cookies, cereal and milk, bread and cheese. They pretended to pay with the pennies, dimes, and nickels.

Soon it was time for Carol and Shannon to go home. Before she left, Shannon secretly stuffed her pocket with Allison's mom's pennies, nickels, and dimes.

Later that day, when Allison put her toys away, she couldn't find her mom's coins. "Where are they?" she thought. "Mom will be disappointed when she finds out I can't find them. And if Shannon or Carol took the money, I'll be mad."

Just then there was a knock on the door. Allison opened the door. There stood Shannon. Before Allison had time to say a word, Shannon said, "I'm sorry, Allison. I took your money. Here is a box of cookies from the "real" store. And here is the 75 cents."

Allison hugged Shannon. God helped Shannon to say "I'm sorry." And God helped Allison to forgive Shannon.

Questions:
1. Who played store? (Allison, Shannon, and Carol)
2. Was Allison sorry for taking the money? (yes)

Activity:
Play "store" together.

Prayer:
Dear God, help me say I'm sorry when I've done something bad. Amen.

JOSEPH TELLS HIS DREAMS
GENESIS 37:1-11

It is not good to brag about yourself. Proverbs 25:27

_____, do you have a favorite shirt or jacket or hat? It's fun to wear it, isn't it?

Joseph had a favorite coat. It was a very pretty coat that had many colors in it. Joseph liked to wear it. His father, Jacob, had given it to him. It was a special coat that Joseph wore when he watched the sheep. Joseph's ten older brothers did not like it when their father gave the coat to Joseph. They were jealous. The brothers did not like Joseph. Each day they all had to work together watching the sheep.

One day, while in the fields, Joseph told his brothers about a dream he'd had. The dream seemed to say that the brothers would some day bow down to Joseph. This made the brothers mad.

Then Joseph had another dream. Again, he told his brothers about it. He said, "I saw the sun, moon, and eleven stars bowing down to me." It was a funny dream. But his family knew that it meant that some day Joseph's father, mother, and brothers would bow down to him.

Now his brothers were even more jealous and mad. They thought Joseph was bragging when he told them his dreams. Even Joseph's father wondered what it all meant.

Maybe Joseph told his brothers the dreams because he wanted them to know how good and important he was going to be. Maybe it would have been better if Joseph had not "bragged" about his dreams to his jealous and angry brothers.

Questions:
1. Who gave Joseph his special coat? (his father, Jacob)
2. Who were jealous of Joseph? (his ten older brothers)

Activities:
1. Name some colors that may have been in Joseph's coat.
2. Draw and color Joseph's coat.

Prayer:
Dear God, help me when I feel like being jealous or braggy. Amen.

THE MEAN BROTHERS
GENESIS 37:12-35

Hatred stirs up trouble. *Proverbs 10:12*

_____, can you count to seventeen? Let's count to seventeen together. Joseph was seventeen years old when his father asked him to do something special for him. He asked Joseph to go see how his shepherd brothers were doing. It was a very long walk. But Joseph was happy to do it for his dad.

Joseph walked for hours. Finally Joseph found his brothers.

"It's our dreamer brother," they said. "Let's get rid of him. Then his 'silly' dreams won't come true. He won't think he's so smart then."

But the oldest brother, Reuben, talked the others out of killing Joseph. Instead, they ripped off his special coat and threw him into a deep, dark, empty hole in the ground. "Please don't leave me here," begged Joseph. But the brothers did not care about their little brother, Joseph. They hated him.

As they sat down to eat dinner, a group of men walked by. The jealous brothers decided to sell Joseph to the men. The brothers laughed as Joseph went off alone with the men.

"Now what should we tell our father about Joseph?" they wondered. "We have to hide what we have done." So they put animal blood on Joseph's coat. Then they showed it to Jacob. They wanted Jacob to think that Joseph was dead. Jacob believed that his son, Joseph, was killed by a wild animal. He was so sad that he could not eat or sleep.

Joseph's brothers did a horrible thing to Joseph *and* to their father.

Questions:

1. Who hated Joseph? (his brothers)

2. Did the brothers lie to their father? (yes)

Activity:

Count to seventeen again. Joseph was a teenager. Name a teenager that you know.

Prayer:

Dear God, please keep me from hatred. I know hating always causes trouble. Amen.

JOSEPH IN JAIL
GENESIS 39:1-23

But the Lord was with Joseph. *Genesis 39:21*

_____, who sold Joseph to the men walking by? Yes, Joseph's hateful and jealous brothers sold him. The men took the seventeen-year-old Joseph to Egypt. Joseph lived there for many years. He was without his father or his little brother, Benjamin. He must have missed them very much.

But the Lord God was with Joseph. He grew older and stronger. He lived with an important leader of Egypt named Potiphar.

Potiphar saw that Joseph loved God. He also saw that God helped Joseph. Potiphar liked Joseph. He asked him to be his best and special servant-helper. Joseph was the manager of everything that Potiphar owned. It was an important job.

But one day Potiphar's wife told a terrible lie about Joseph. So Potiphar put Joseph into jail. Joseph had done nothing wrong, but now he was in a dirty, creepy jail.

The Lord God helped Joseph. He showed him kindness. The prison warden liked Joseph. He chose Joseph to take care of all the other prisoners. And God helped Joseph do a good job. God was with Joseph in some sad and lonely places.

Questions:
1. What important leader did Joseph live with after he was taken to Egypt? (Potiphar)
2. Who lied about Joseph? (Potiphar's wife)
3. What job did the prison warden give Joseph? (the job of taking care of all the prisoners)

Activity:
Sing the song "Jesus Loves Me," but change the words to "God is with me, this I know. . . ."

Prayer:
Dear God, You helped Joseph in some hard and lonely times. Please help me, too. Amen.

JOSEPH GETS OUT OF JAIL
GENESIS 40, 41

It is God who makes us able to do all that we do. 2 Corinthians 3:5

_____, where did the Egyptian leader Potiphar send Joseph? Yes, he sent him to jail. But God was with Joseph while he was in jail. Joseph had an important job helping the warden (the boss-leader of the jail) with the other prisoners.

One day, two fellow prisoners had dreams, but they did not know what they meant. God helped Joseph understand the dreams. Soon one of the men got out of prison.

"Please remember me," begged Joseph. "Tell the king about me so I can get out, too. Tell him that I've done nothing wrong." But the man forgot all about Joseph. And Joseph stayed in jail two more long years.

Then the king had a dream. The king was told about Joseph and how he had told the men in prison what their dreams meant. The king called Joseph out of the jail. God helped Joseph know the meaning of the king's dream. "There will be seven years of good crops. We will have lots of food for everyone. Then we will have seven years of bad crops. The people will get very hungry. So I have an idea. Let's save the food during the years of good crops. We can keep it in a safe place. Then there will be food for everyone to eat in the seven bad years."

"Great idea!" said the king. "I want you to take care of it all." It was a special job. People bowed down to Joseph. Only the king of Egypt was more important than Joseph. God helped Joseph do a good job as a new leader of Egypt.

Questions:
1. Who told the king what his dream meant? (Joseph)
2. Did Joseph get out of jail? (yes)

Activities:
1. Count to seven.
2. Pretend to bow down to the leader, Joseph.

Prayer:
Dear God, You help us do all that we need to do. Thank You. Amen.

THE FAMILY TOGETHER AGAIN
GENESIS 42-46

Be kind and loving to each other. Forgive each other.

Ephesians 4:32

_____, what do you want when you are hungry? Yes, you want food, don't you? During the seven years of bad crops, Joseph's father and brothers ran out of food. They were hungry.

One day Jacob told his ten sons to go get some food in Egypt. So the brothers went down to Egypt. When they arrived in Egypt, they went to Joseph. Joseph knew it was his brothers. But they did not know it was Joseph. They bought grain and went back to Jacob.

But soon they ate all the food and were hungry again. So they went again to Egypt. This time they took Joseph's little brother, Benjamin. Joseph had dinner with all eleven brothers this time. Still they did not know that this ruler of Egypt was the same brother that they had treated so mean.

After awhile, Joseph could keep his secret no longer. He started to cry. "I am your brother, Joseph," he said. "Tell me, how is my father?"

"Oh, no!" thought the brothers. "Now Joseph will pay us back for being so mean to him."

But Joseph said, "Do not be afraid. God is the one who sent me here. You tried to hurt me, but God turned your bad into good. Now go get my father. I want to see him."

So the brothers hurried home to their father, Jacob. He was surprised and happy to find out that his beloved son, Joseph, was still alive. Then Jacob brought the whole family back with him to Egypt. When Joseph saw his dad, he cried. They hugged each other for a long time. God brought the whole family back together again.

Questions:
1. Did Joseph's brothers know it was Joseph? (no)
2. Did Joseph forgive his brothers? (yes)
3. Was the whole family together again? (yes)

Activity:
Hug your child like Jacob hugged Joseph.

Prayer:
Dear God, thank You for bringing Joseph back together with his family. I know You are happy when families love and forgive each other. Amen.

BABY IN A BOAT
EXODUS 1:22—2:4

It was by faith that Moses' parents hid him. *Hebrews 11:23*

_____, do you like babies? They are cute and cuddly, aren't they? A long time ago in Egypt, a special baby boy was born. He was cute and cuddly. His mother looked at her son's big brown eyes and soft little mouth. But in her heart was sadness, also. Pharaoh, the bad king of Egypt, said that every Hebrew newborn baby boy had to be thrown into the river. The Hebrew people were slaves in Egypt, and the king was afraid that the baby boys would one day grow into men who might try to leave Egypt.

God loved and protected the Hebrew people. He helped the baby's mother hide her baby from the king for a long time. But soon the baby's mother could hide him from the king no longer. What would she do?

One day God gave her an idea. She found a wicker basket and covered it so that water could not come in it. Then she wrapped her baby in blankets, and put him into the small basket-boat. She leaned over and kissed him on his soft little cheek.

Then the mother hid her baby in the tall weeds by the Nile River. She asked his big sister, Miriam, to watch him from a little way off. Then they waited. They waited and watched to see what God would do next.

Questions:

1. What did the king say about newborn Hebrew baby boys? (They all must be thrown into the river.)

2. What did the baby's mother do? (She made a little basket-boat for him and hid him in the tall weeds by the river.)

3. Who watched the baby? (his big sister)

Activities:

1. Show your child a photo of when he(she) was born. Ask him(her) to point to the cute nose, mouth, ears, etc.

2. For an extended activity, cut out baby pictures from magazines. Attach the pictures to a page including his(her) baby photo. Display the finished product for all to enjoy.

Prayer:

Dear God, thank You for the good idea that You gave to the baby's mother. She had faith that You would take care of her baby.

WHO FOUND THE BABY?
EXODUS 2:5-10

Trust him (God), and he will take care of you. *Psalm 37:5*

Miriam watched her baby brother as he floated in the boat. She made sure he got milk when he was hungry. She probably whispered to him when he cried. Always she was careful to hide if someone came near.

While the parents waited and big sister watched, the daughter of the bad king Pharaoh came down to take a bath in the river. As they were walking by the side of the river, one of her maids saw the basket-boat floating in the tall weeds. She hurried to show it to Pharaoh's daughter.

How surprised she was when she looked inside! There was a beautiful baby! He was crying! Pharaoh's daughter felt sorry for the baby. She was much kinder than her father, Pharaoh.

She said, "Oh, this baby is one of the Hebrew's children." She knew her jealous father wanted to get rid of all these babies.

Just then, Miriam ran from her hiding place. "Shall I get a Hebrew mother to take care of the child for you?" the baby's sister asked.

"Oh, yes," said Pharaoh's daughter. Miriam ran to tell her mother all that had happened. Now the baby's mother could nurse and take care of him until he was old enough to live in the palace. After several years, Pharaoh's daughter adopted him as her own son and named him Moses.

God took good care of baby Moses. Moses' family trusted God. _____, we can trust God to care for us, too.

Questions:
1. Who watched the baby in the tall weeds? (his sister, Miriam)

2. Who found and adopted the baby? (Pharaoh's daughter)

3. What did she name the baby boy? (Moses)

Activity:
Get a little basket or box. Put a little doll into it. Pretend that it is baby Moses floating on the water.

Prayer:
Dear God, Moses' parents trusted You to keep him safe. I will trust You also to keep me safe at home, school, church, and play. Amen.

IT'S ON FIRE!
EXODUS 3:1-13

God will be with you everywhere you go.
Joshua 1:9

When Moses grew up, he moved away from Egypt. One day he was out in the fields taking care of the sheep. "What is this?" Moses whispered. "The bush looks like it's on fire, but it isn't burning up."

"Moses, Moses," called a voice from the bush.

"Here I am," answered Moses.

"Don't come any closer. This is God talking to you. I want to tell you a special secret." Moses covered his face and waited for God to share the secret with him.

"I have heard the prayers of my people who are having trouble in Egypt. Moses, I want you to get them out."

"But God," Moses said, "I'm afraid. It's too hard."

"You can do it, Moses," God said. "I will be with you."

_____, sometimes, like Moses, you and I might think we cannot do what God wants us to do. But God promises that He will be with us, to help us everywhere we go.

Questions:
1. What did Moses see? (a bush that was on fire but that was not burning up)
2. Who talked to Moses? (God)

Activities:
1. Name some things you might think you cannot do (ideas: share my new toys with a friend; wait to eat lunch until Mom says; go to school by myself; obey when it's time to go to sleep).
2. Say the Joshua 1:9 verse together.

Prayer:
Dear God, I need Your help. Sometimes it is hard for me to share, wait, or obey. But I know that You will be with me and help me always. Amen.

WHO MADE YOUR MOUTH?
EXODUS 3:11-14; 4:1-17

"Please, Lord, send someone else." *Exodus 4:13*

"Go, get my people out of Egypt. And re-member, Moses, I will be with you," said God.

"What if they don't believe me?" asked Moses.

"See that stick in your hand? Throw it on the ground." When Moses threw it down, it became a real live snake. "Now reach out and grab it by the tail," said God. Moses did and it was a stick again. God showed Moses that He was strong enough to help him in Egypt.

_____, can you count to five? 1-2-3-4-5. Five times Moses told God, "I can't do it!" Every time God listened.

"I will help you," God promised.

"I don't know the right words to say," said Moses. "I talk funny."

"Moses, who made your mouth?" asked God. "Now, go and I will tell you what to say."

Again Moses begged, "Please, God, send someone else."

Then God was sad with Moses' words. "Your brother, Aaron, talks well," said God. "He'll come with you. I will tell *you* what to say, you tell Aaron, and then Aaron will talk to the people. Now take your walking stick. You will use it to do special things."

God had an important job for Moses to do.

Questions:"
1. What happened when Moses threw his stick on the ground? (It became a snake.)
2. What was Moses' important job? (to get the people out of Egypt)

Activity:
Name or point to the parts of the body, saying, "God made my _____." ("God made my mouth, . . . nose, . . . eyes, . . . tummy, . . . foot, . . .etc.")

Prayer:
Dear God, You made Moses' mouth. You made my mouth. Help me to obey You with my whole body, including my mouth. Amen.

LET THE PEOPLE GO!
EXODUS 5:1-6, 9

"I am the Lord, God all Powerful." *Exodus 6:2, 3*

_____, do you remember the names of the two brothers God sent to Egypt? Yes, Moses and Aaron were their names. After Moses and Aaron talked with the poor, hurting Israelite people, they went to see the king of Egypt.

"The Lord, the God of Israel, told us to tell you to 'Let the people go!'" they said to the king.

"Are you joking? Who is the Lord? Why should I obey Him?" asked the king. "I don't even know the Lord? I will *not* let these people go."

Moses and Aaron tried to tell the king what God wanted. But the king said, "Why do you want to take these people away from their work? Maybe they're getting lazy. I'll just have to make them work harder." So the king told the bosses to hit the people and make them work longer and harder.

"Now they won't have time to listen to Moses and Aaron," he said. The king was a very mean man. He did not care about God at all.

"God, why did You send me here?" asked Moses. "The king is hurting the people more. And now the people won't even listen to Aaron or me."

Then God said, "It seems like it's not working. But you watch me! You will see how great I am! The king will change his mind. I will get these people out of Egypt and into their own country."

Questions:
1. Who talked to the king? (Moses and Aaron)
2. Did the king let the people go? (no)

Activity:
Draw a picture of the "mean" king's face when he said, "NO!"

Prayer:
Dear God, some people, like the Egyptian king, don't love or know You. But I know You, and I love You. I believe that You are the God who has all power. Amen.

THE STINKY WATER
EXODUS 7:14-24

The wicked man has no respect for God.
Psalm 36:1

_____, have you ever been fishing? Have you ever smelled a stinky dead fish? Listen to a story about lots of smelly fish.

Moses and Aaron came to the king today. But the king would not listen to them. "No," he said, "the people cannot go."

Every morning the king went down to the river. So God told Moses to meet the king by the river. "Tell him again that I, God, say to 'Let my people go.' If he doesn't let my people go I will make all the water turn to blood," said God.

When Moses and Aaron talked to the king, he said, "No." So the water turned to blood. The fish died. The river started to stink. The Egyptian people did not have clean water to wash with. They could not even take a drink. It was hard for the people without water.

But the bad king did not care about God or Moses or even his own people. He was a very wicked man.

Questions:
1. Where did the king go every morning? (to the river)
2. Who told the king to "Let my people go"? (God through Moses and Aaron)
3. Did the king let the people go? (no)
4. What happened to the water? (God turned it to blood.)

Activity:
Name different ways that we use water (ideas: to wash hands; to take a bath; to drink; to cook food; to swim).

Prayer:
Dear God, Moses and Aaron obeyed You. They did what You said to do even when the king would not listen. Help me to do what You tell me to do (in the Bible) even when someone else doesn't listen and even when they make fun of me. Amen.

FROGS AND FLIES: BUGS AND BOILS
EXODUS 7:25—10:20

They (liars) say one thing and mean another. *Psalm 12:2*

_____, can you count to seven? Seven days after the fish died in the stinky river, God told Moses to talk to the king again. "If he does not change his mind and let my people go, then lots of frogs will come into Egypt," said God. "You can tell the king this."

But the king did not change his mind. And the frogs came. They jumped everywhere—in the yards, in the houses, in the churches, in the marketplace. At dinner time, they jumped into the frying pans. At night the people found frogs under their blankets. Even when the king's men tried to talk, the frogs jumped into their mouths.

So the king said, "Take the frogs away, and the people can go!" But the king lied. He would not let the people go when the frogs left.

Then tiny bugs came on the Egyptian people and their animals. They itched all over. But still the king said, "NO!"

Buzzing flies flew into Egypt. The flies were messing up everything. The king hated them. "Get rid of them, and you can go," he said. But again he lied.

The mean king did not care about God or anyone else. All the farm animals died with a disease. And then hurting sores, called boils, came on the skin of all the people. But still the king promised one thing and did another. He lied. He would not let the people go.

Questions:

1. What jumped into the people's beds and into their pans when they were cooking? (frogs)

2. Who lied? (the king)

Activity:

1. Color this frog green. Make a buzzing sound like a fly.

2. Read and discuss the verse above, Psalm 12:2.

Prayer:

Dear God, the king lied to Moses. You want people to say what they really mean. Help me to always tell the truth. Amen.

MOSES HAD FAITH
EXODUS 9:1—11:8; 12:29-33

It was by faith that Moses was not afraid of the king's anger.
Hebrews 11:27

Even after all the sad things happened, the king would not let the Israelite people go. Moses came to him again. "God says that if you don't let the people go, a very bad hail storm will come down on you."

"NO!" repeated the king. So hail came down. Houses were crushed. Trees fell down. People were hurt and killed.

The king was sad. "I've been wrong," he said. "I will let you go."

But when the storm stopped, the king did not let the people go. Then big loud bugs called locusts covered the ground. They ate all the food. Again the king lied to Moses. A darkness like never before came over everything. No one could see to cook or read or write. Still the king would not let the people go. "Moses, get out of here!" shouted the king. "I never want to see you again. If you come back, you will die!"

Then God said to Moses, "I have one more way to change the king's mind. After this, he *will* let them go."

In the middle of the night, the oldest boy in every Egyptian family died. All the mothers and fathers cried. The king's people said, "Hurry up and let those Israelite people go. We are too sad to have anything else happen to us." Then the king's son died, too. So the king called Moses. "GO! Take your people and leave!"

_____, finally the king let the people go.

Questions:
1. What were the big loud bugs called? (locusts)
2. Who finally said, "Go" instead of "No"? (the king)

Activity:
Turn the light off for a moment and close your eyes. Discuss how it would be if there was complete darkness everywhere.

Prayer:
Dear God, Moses did what you said even when the king kept saying "No." He had faith in You. I want to have faith in You, too. Amen.

THE LONGEST PARADE
EXODUS 12:37-40; 13:17—14:3

He led them with a cloud by day.
And he led them at night by the light of a fire. *Psalm 78:14*

_____, do you like to watch parades? Moses and Aaron led the Israelite people in the longest parade ever. Fathers, mothers, children, and grandparents marched in the parade. Sheep, little lambs, goats, and cows marched in the parade. They were all very happy and excited to be marching together, away from the mean king of Egypt.

God told Moses where to lead the parade. During the day God led them by a special cloud that moved in the blue sky. At night a special cloud of fire moved in the dark sky. When these clouds moved, the people moved. When the clouds stopped, the people stopped.

Soon Moses and the people heard a noise that sounded like loud thunder. When they turned they saw the king of Egypt with all his army chasing after them.

"Oh, no! What are we going to do?" they cried.

Then Moses said, "Don't be afraid! God has a plan. Stand still and watch what God is going to do. You will be surprised! He will keep us safe."

Questions:

1. Who marched in the long parade? (moms, dads, children, animals)

2. Who chased after the people? (the king and his army)

3. What did Moses tell the frightened Israelite people? ("Don't be afraid. God has a plan.")

Activities:

1. Use little toy people or blocks to make a pretend parade.

2. Name some things that you see in a parade.

Prayer:

Dear God, Moses said, "Don't be afraid." But it looked very scary to the people. Sometimes things look scary to me, too. That's when I need Your help. Thank You for always being there to help me. Amen.

63

GOD'S PLAN
EXODUS 14:15-22

Come and see what God has done. He turned the sea into dry land.

Psalm 66:5, 6

_____, how could the people get away from the king and his army? Moses and the people stood beside a big lake called the Red Sea. And way down the road, the mean king and his army chased after them. They were afraid.

But God said, "Moses, listen to my plan. Lift your stick and hold it over the water. When you hold up your stick, the water will split. The water will be like walls on each side. There will be dry land where water used to be. Take the long parade of people and walk on the dry land."

God had more to His plan. He took the cloud that was in front of the people and put it in back of them. The king and his army could not see them. All night it kept the king's army and God's people apart. So the Israelite people all walked safely across dry land.

When the army tried to follow the people across the path in the big lake, the water came crashing on top of them. But Moses and the people stayed safe! God said that He would take care of them. And He did! It took a long time for all those people to walk across the big lake, but God kept them safe until the last little lamb was safely on the other side. They did not even get muddy!

Questions:
1. Who had a plan to help the Israelite people? (God)
2. What happened to the water when Moses obeyed God and held

out the stick over the water? (The water split and made a path of dry land.)

Activity:
Talk about what happens when water and dirt come together (mud). What usually happens when you walk in mud? Discuss the fact that the Israelite people did not get wet or muddy.

Prayer:
Dear God, You had a great plan to keep the Israelites safe. You can do anything. Amen.

MIRIAM LEADS A CHOIR
EXODUS 15:1-21

It is good to sing praises to our God.
Psalm 147:1

_____, do you like to
sing? God likes to hear our songs. God is
the one who makes our mouths and throats.
He is the one who makes us so we can sing.
Moses and all the people sang this spe-
cial song of thanksgiving to God:
"I sing to the Lord.
He saved me from the king.
He is my God.
He makes me sing."
They were so happy to be safe. After
more than 400 years of hard work, they
were finally away from the mean people
who hurt them.

Miriam, Moses' and Aaron's sister, took a tambourine in her hand.
She played it and led a big women's choir. The choir sang beautiful
songs to God.

God loves to hear us sing to Him. God is the one who gives us
music. Isn't it fun to sing songs to God?

Questions:
1. Who makes us so we can sing? (God)
2. Why did the people sing happy songs to God? (God had saved
them from the bad king.)

Activity:
1. Take a key ring with several keys on it. Shake it. The sound it
makes sounds something like a tambourine.
2. Shake your "tambourine" of keys while you sing a happy song to
God.

Prayer:
Dear God, I will sing a song to You at home and at church. Singing
makes You happy. Singing songs to You is fun. Thank You for music.
Amen.

FOOD FROM HEAVEN
EXODUS 16:1-5

He rained manna down on them to eat. Psalm 78:24

Moses and the people had been away from the bad king for about six weeks. _____, do you remember when God helped them get away from the king? God made a pathway in the water of the Red Sea. Later He gave them good water to drink. But the people forgot how God helped them. They started to cry. They were grouchy.

"Here we are way out in the desert with no food or meat to eat," they said to Moses and Aaron. "We're all going to die. Why didn't God just leave us in Egypt? We could have died there, you know."

Then God said, "Moses, I'm going to send food to you. It will come down from the sky like rain. Every day the food will come. Tell each family to go get enough food for the meals for that day. Tell them that on Friday of every week to take enough food for two days. If you obey me, you will always have food to eat."

God heard the people's crying and grumbling. Then he told Moses about His special plan to feed all the people. God always took care of His people, but it seemed like they had a hard time believing. This made God very unhappy. It makes God unhappy when we don't trust in Him to do the things that He has promised.

Questions:

1. Why were the Israelites grouchy? (They had no food to eat.)

2. How was God going to give them food? (It would come down like rain from heaven.)

Activity:

1. Pretend to be the Israelite people waiting for the food to come out of the sky. Eat crackers and pretend that they have just dropped out of the sky.

2. Name food that you like to eat.

Prayer:

Dear God, the people needed to eat to stay healthy. You gave them food. Thank You for my food, also. Amen.

LET'S HELP MOSES
EXODUS 17:8-15

Help each other with your troubles. *Galatians 6:2*

_____, put your arms straight up in the air. Count to ten. Are your arms tired? No? Count to ten again. Are your arms starting to get tired? If you held your arms up like this all day, you would get tired, wouldn't you? Listen to a story about Moses and his tired arms.

One day an army of people called Amalekites came up behind Moses and the people on the road. The Amalekites started to fight with the people at the end of the long parade. Moses saw what happened. So he called a good man named Joshua to come and talk with him.

"Joshua, choose some strong men. Then get ready to fight against the Amalekites." Aaron and a man named Hur went with Moses to the hill. When Moses held his hands up high, Joshua and the Israelite men won the fight. But when Moses' hands came down to rest, the Amalekites won the fight. Aaron and Hur saw what was happening.

"Moses is getting very tired," they said. "What can we do?" Then God gave them an idea. They moved a rock for Moses to sit on. Then Aaron held up one of Moses' arms and Hur held up the other arm. They helped their leader Moses. And the Israelites won the fight. Aaron and Hur pleased God because they helped Moses when he needed it.

Questions:
1. Who started a fight with the people? (the Amalekites)
2. How did Aaron and Hur help Moses? (They held Moses' arms up when he got tired.)

Activity:
Name ways to help people when they are tired (ideas: get diaper for mom to change baby; help carry the books and Bibles to church; help set the table; play quietly while tired mommy takes a rest).

Prayer:
Dear God, Aaron and Hur helped Moses when he needed it. I can help other people when they need it, too. Please help me. Amen.

ROGER IS A HELPER
EXODUS 17:1-13

So let us try to do what makes peace and helps one another.

Romans 14:19

"Mom," yelled Roger. "I'm thirsty. Get me a drink!"

"I'm feeding baby Allison right now. We'll have lunch when I'm finished," answered Mom.

Roger kicked his toy truck. He did not want to wait. He thought his new baby sister, Allison, took *all* of his Mom's time. He felt grouchy.

"Mom," Roger yelled again. "I said I'm thirsty—I'm hungry, too! Do you have to feed Allison now?"

"Yes, I do," said Mom. "I know you're hungry. I know you're thirsty, too. But, Roger, so am I. And I'm very tired. I didn't get much sleep last night. I would like to have your help. Then we could have lunch sooner. You could help me by being quiet so Allison can go to sleep. And you could also help by bringing the baby's diaper to me."

Roger stood in the doorway for a minute. He heard what his mother said. He looked at her in the rocking chair. She looked tired. Then he remembered the story about Moses and his tired arms. Aaron and Hur helped Moses when he needed it.

"Well, OK, Mom," he said. "Here's the diaper. I'll be quiet now. Do you want me to go get the bread down so we can make sandwiches?"

"That would be nice," said Mom. "You're a big helper. Thank you."

Questions:

1. Why was Roger grouchy? (He wanted a drink and some food.)
2. What was Mom doing? (feeding baby Allison)
3. Who decided to help Mom? (Roger)

Activities:

1. Fill in the blank with your name. _____ is a helper.
2. Name the ways that you were helpful today. (Parent: Help your child think of the ways she was helpful. Praise her for her helpfulness.)

Prayer:

Dear God, please help me to be a helper to Mom and Dad. Amen.

MOSES CLIMBS A MOUNTAIN
EXODUS 19:1-8

Then Moses went up on the mountain to God. *Exodus 19:3*

_____ _____, have you ever seen a real mountain? See the tall mountain in this picture? All the people with Moses traveled in the long parade. They stopped to "camp out" by a very big mountain. The mountain was called Mount Sinai.

God talked to Moses from the mountain. "Tell all the people that I helped them get away from the bad king and his army. I gave them water to drink and crackers and quail to eat. I, God, am the one who brought them here. Tell them to always do what I say and I will take care of them. They will be my very special people.

So Moses walked down the side of the mountain. Moses was a good climber. He called a meeting of all the leaders of the people. He told them what God said.

"We will do everything God tells us to do," they promised.

So Moses climbed back up the mountain to tell God what the people said. Moses cared about the people. But he loved God more. He told the people about God. God was getting ready to tell Moses some very special words. These words would help the people to live a happy life—a life of loving and obeying God.

Questions:

1. Where did the people "camp out"? (by a very big mountain, Mount Sinai)

2. Who talked to Moses from the mountain? (God)

3. What did God say? (I am the one who helps you. Do what I say and I will help you always.)

Activities:

1. Pretend you're climbing a mountain with rocks and steep sides.

2. Find mountain pictures in a magazine.

Prayer:

Dear God, thank You for taking care of the Israelite people. And thank You for taking care of me. Amen.

TEN SPECIAL RULES
EXODUS 20:1-17

Help me want to obey your rules. *Psalm 119:36*

Moses climbed to the top of the mountain to meet with God. He stayed there for 40 days and nights. While he was camping on the mountain, God gave him ten rules to help the people live a safe and good life. "I am the one who helped you get away from the bad king," God said. "I have taken care of you before; and I will take care of you again. Believe in me. Listen and obey these words of mine:

1. Do not worship or pray to any other god but me.

2. Do not ever think that anything is more important than me.

3. Do not call out God's name by swearing or cussing. Only use God's name lovingly.

4. Do not work on the seventh day of the week. Work for six days and rest and worship God on the seventh day.

5. Obey and honor your mom and dad.

6. Do not kill anyone.

7. Do not live with a man/woman you are not married to.

8. Do not steal.

9. Do not tell lies.

10. Do not want to take a friend's things just because what he has is better or nicer than what you have.

God wrote these ten special rules on the stones with His finger. (Have you ever seen writing on rocks or stones?)

God helped Moses understand the rules. We call these special rules the Ten Commandments.

_____, God gave these rules to us because He loves us and wants us to be safe and happy.

Questions:
1. Where did God meet with Moses? (on the mountain)
2. Who wrote on the stones with His finger? (God)

Activities:
1. Count to ten.
2. Name two of the ten commandments God gave to Moses and us.

Prayer:
Dear God, I know that these rules are to help me live a safe and good life. These rules also help me to see that I need Your help. Please help me obey them. Thank You. Amen.

THE GOLD CALF
EXODUS 32:1-18

You must not make any idols. Don't make something
that looks like anything on the earth. *Deuteronomy 5:8*

"Where is Moses?" asked the people. "He is supposed to be our
leader. But where is he now?" They were tired of waiting for Moses
to come down from the mountain. So they asked Aaron to make them
a new and different god to follow.

Aaron had promised to worship and do what the Lord God wanted.
But he "forgot" the promise. "OK, let's make an idol," said Aaron.
"Give me all of your gold earrings. I will melt them and make a statue
of a baby cow."

The people danced around the golden calf. They sang to it. They
worshipped it. But the gold calf idol could not talk back.

God saw what the people did. He was sad. God said, "Do not worship or pray to any other god." The people acted like God was not even
alive. What they did was called "sin."

Moses stayed on the mountain with
God for 40 days. When he returned and
saw the people praying to the golden
calf, he was very sad. Moses faced the
singing, dancing people. "Anyone who
wants to follow and worship the Lord
God, come stand by me," he shouted.

_____, it is very
sad when people "forget" God and
refuse to do what He says. The people had a choice to make. We have
a choice, too. Let's choose to pray, believe, and worship God.

Questions:
1. Who helped the people make a gold calf? (Aaron)
2. Was it wrong to worship the gold calf idol? (yes)

Activity:
Take ice cubes and melt them. Pour them into another mold and
freeze. Explain that when gold rings and earrings get very hot they
melt, also. Then they can be shaped into something different.

Prayer:
Dear God, nothing is more important than worshipping and believing You. I choose to sing and pray to You. Amen.

TWO NEW STONES
EXODUS 34:1-35

The Lord is kind, has great love, forgives people for wrong and sin.

Exodus 34:6, 7

When Moses returned and saw the people disobeying God by dancing and singing around the gold calf idol, he threw down the two stones God had given him. CRASH! BANG! They broke into little pieces.

But God came to Moses and said, "Get two more stones ready. Come back up to the mountain, and I will write my words on them again."

So Moses climbed the mountain again. God came to him in a cloud. "I am kind," said God. "I care about the people even when they disobey. I do not get mad quickly. I have a lot of love. When people do wrong things, I forgive them. But I do not let people keep doing wrong things and disobeying. I show I love them by punishing them.

Moses bowed before God. He was thankful for God's love and forgiveness.

_____, to forgive means to stop being mad at another person for the wrong or sinful things he did. To punish means that when a person disobeys, then he may have to lose something (like he will not get to play outside); or be hurt (he might have to sit quietly in a chair). If a person is punished, then he might not go against the rules and do the wrong thing again. If he is *not* punished, he might think it is OK to disobey again. God loved the people too much to let them keep disobeying.

Questions:
1. Who broke the stones? (Moses)
2. Did God write on new stones? (yes)

Activities:
1. Point to the two stones in the picture.
2. Color the stones on this page.

Prayer:
Dear God, You said that You are kind and loving. You said You forgive us. I believe this is what You are like. And I love You. Amen.

WHO TOOK ERIC'S LUNCH?
HEBREWS 12:4-11; EXODUS 32:1-36

The Lord corrects those he loves. *Hebrews 12:6*

_____, what do you like to have for lunch? Every day Eric took his favorite food in a bag lunch to school. One morning, Eric put on his coat, grabbed his bag lunch, and hurried to the bus stop. He knew that by 11:00 he would be very hungry.

"Oh, no," thought Eric as he looked out the bus window. "Please don't sit by me." He watched Butch climb up the steps of the bus. Butch walked right over and sat down in the seat next to Eric. Eric pushed his bag lunch under the seat with his foot. But when the bus turned the next corner, Eric's bag lunch fell out from under the seat.

"So," said Butch in a mean voice, "you brought me lunch again today." He grabbed Eric's bag lunch from the floor.

"No, that is *my* lunch," said Eric quietly. "I brought it from home for *me* to eat. You should get your own lunch."

"Why should I get my own lunch when you have one for me?" yelled Butch.

"But then I get hungry," said Eric. "This is three days in a row that you've taken my lunch."

Butch just laughed. "You're a baby! Baby Eric! He's so hungry!"

Just then the bus stopped. The bus driver turned around. He looked at Eric's sad face. Then he looked at Butch's laughing mean face. "I heard everything," said the bus driver. "Butch, give that lunch back to Eric. When we get to school, I will have a talk with your teacher. You have been taking what is not yours. That is wrong. You will be punished so you will learn not to do it again."

Questions:
1. Who took Eric's lunch? (Butch)
2. Was it wrong for Butch to take Eric's lunch? (yes)

Activity:
Make a bag lunch for today's or tomorrow's lunch time.

Prayer:
Dear God, help me never to take what is not mine. Amen.

A NEW LEADER
JOSHUA 1:1-9, 16-18

God has said, "I will never leave you."

Hebrews 13:5

_____, who led the people out of Egypt and away from the bad king? Yes, it was Moses. Moses was a special man of God. He loved and prayed to God. God helped him to be a good leader.

When Moses died, the people were very sad. They cried for 30 days. "Now who will be our leader?" they wondered.

Then God said, "Joshua, you are the new leader. I know it is a *very* big job. But be brave! Don't be afraid! I will be with you all the time. I will never leave you!"

So the people followed their new leader, Joshua. "God helped Moses when he was leader," the people said. "Now God will help our new leader, Joshua. We will do whatever Joshua tells us to do."

Joshua told the people that God would keep His promise to give them new land and new homes. They believed Joshua. They believed God.

Joshua loved and prayed to God for help in leading the people, just like Moses did. God promised that He would never leave Joshua alone.

God will never leave you and me alone, either.

Questions:
1. Who was the new leader? (Joshua)
3. Who promised never to leave Joshua alone and promises never to leave us alone? (God)

Activity:
1. Say the Hebrews 13:5 verse from the top of the page together.
2. Make a puzzle by writing the above verse on a large piece of paper and then cutting the page into puzzle pieces. Now put the puzzle together.

Prayer:
Dear God, You said You would never leave Joshua. I know You will never leave me, either. Thank You. Amen.

NO ONE GOT MUDDY!
JOSHUA 4:1-24

The Lord did this so all people would know he has great power.
Joshua 4:24

_____, who was the people's new leader? Yes, Joshua was their new leader. Joshua came out to talk to the people. He said, "Get ready! Tomorrow God is going to do exciting and wonderful things for you."

It was time for the people to go into their new land. God had promised this land to them. But the new land was on the other side of the river. How could they get there? How could they cross that river? But God had an idea. It was a good idea.

He said, "Carry my special box at the front of the line. When you put your foot into the river, the water will go away." So the people stepped into the river. Do you know what happened? The water parted. God made a dry path in the middle of the river. The people walked on the path. They didn't even get muddy! Joshua was right. God did an exciting and wonderful thing for the people.

God did the same thing for the moms and dads of these people many years before. He stopped the water so the people could get away from the bad king of Egypt. Do you remember that story? Now he stopped the water so they could go to the new land. God helped them when they needed it. "God wants *all* people to know how big and strong He is," said Joshua.

God helps us when we need it. He shows us how strong He is.

Questions:
1. Who said, "God will do exciting things for you"? (Joshua)
2. How did they the people get across the water? (God made a dry path in the river.)
3. Did they get muddy? (no)
4. Why did God do this? (to show how strong He is)

Activities:
1. March around the room. Pretend that you're crossing the dry river.
2. Parents: Explain to your child that God's special box was a box that contained the stone tablets that God had given to Moses with the Ten Commandments written on them.

Prayer:
Dear God, You are very strong. You are very powerful! Amen.

THE MARCH
JOSHUA 6:1-27

It was by faith that the walls of Jericho fell. *Hebrews 11:30*

_____, do you like to march? It's fun to march around like a soldier, isn't it? One day, the Israelite people went on a march. It was God's idea. It was His way to help the people get into one of the cities in their new land.

God said, "Joshua, take all your soldiers. March together around the city every day. Do this for six days. On the seventh day, march around the city seven times. Blow seven trumpets and shout! The big gates and walls around the city will fall down. Then all your people can walk into the city. It will be your city!"

So Joshua did just what God said to do. The soldier men walked around the city for seven days. On the seventh day, they marched around it seven times. They shouted together, and the walls fell down. CRASH! BANG!

It all happened just like God said it would! God's idea worked. God helped Joshua. Soon everyone heard all about Joshua and the people.

Questions:

1. Whose idea was it to march around the city? (God's)

2. How many days did they march? (seven)

3. What happened on the seventh day? (The walls around the city fell down.)

4. Did it happen like God said it would? (yes)

Activities:

1. March around the house.

2. Make a trumpet out of a rolled piece of paper or an empty paper towel core.

Prayer:

Dear God, Your idea was a good one. It worked! Help me to remember that *all* Your ideas (the words in the Bible) are good ones. Amen.

JOSHUA SAYS GOOD-BYE
JOSHUA 23, 24

You must choose for yourselves whom you will serve. *Joshua 24:15*

Joshua was getting ready to go live with God in heaven. He was old. He had been a good leader. He said to the people, "It's almost time for me to die. God has done wonderful and special things for you. God gave you the new land with your new homes.

"Now, people, you decide. You make up your mind. Will you choose to love, pray, and sing to God?"

The people said, "We have decided. We will love, pray, and sing to God only. We will not pray to anyone else."

So Joshua wrote all these things down in a special book. "These are very special and important words. Always remember that you have promised to love and pray to God. Now it's time for me to say good-bye."

_____, you and I can make up our minds to love, pray, and sing to God, too. We must choose if we want to believe and follow God.

Questions:
1. Who was going to live with God in heaven? (Joshua)
2. Who always keeps His promises? (God)
3. What does "decide" mean? (to make up your mind)
4. What did the people decide to do? (to love, sing, and pray to God)

Activities:
1. Name some promises you have made (ideas: promise to do what my mom or dad says; promise to pick up my toys; promise not to cry when I go to preschool or church school).
2. Put your hands together (like a book). Pretend to read and sing to God.

Prayer:
Dear God, I want to love, sing, and pray to You. Help me to keep my promise. Amen.

DAVEY'S OPERATION
JUDGES 6—7

Then God will strengthen you with his own great power.
Colossians 1:11

Davey had a bad sore throat. It was hard to eat. It was even hard to drink. Davey's throat hurt so much that he felt like crying. He had had a sore throat six times just since his five-year-old birthday. His doctor said that he needed to go to the hospital to have an "operation."

"Mom, what's an operation?" asked Davey.

"Operation is another name for surgery," answered Mom. "Most of the time surgery is done in a hospital. The nurses and doctors put you to sleep. It's a special kind of sleep. Then they work (or operate) on the part of your body that hurts. Your throat hurts because something is wrong. So an operation will help to fix it."

"Will you be with me?" Davey asked.

"I will be with you in your room before you go to sleep and after you wake up," said Mom. But God will be with you even when the doctor is working on your throat.

"I'm scared," said Davey.

"I know you feel afraid, Davey," said Mom. "Remember the stories of Moses and Joshua leading the Israelite people to the promised land? There were many times when they felt afraid. They didn't think they were strong enough to take care of all those people. But they didn't have to do it alone. God was with them. And God will be with you, Davey. He will help you to be strong."

"Mom, can we pray to God right now?" asked Davey.

"Sure," said Mom. Just then, Daddy walked into Davey's room. After they prayed together, Dad whispered in Davey's ear, "I love you." Then Davey smiled as he remembered that God would help him.

_____, God will help you, too.

Questions:
   1. Who was going to have an "operation"? (Davey)
   2. Who would help Davey when he did not feel strong? (God)
Activities:
   1. Name a doctor that you know. Pray for him or her.
   2. Take your child's pulse.
Prayer:
   Dear God, thank You for being strong when I feel weak. Amen.

A GIRL NAMED RUTH
RUTH 1, 2

Yes, I am sure that nothing can separate us
from the love God has for us. *Romans 8:38*

_____, there are only two books in the Bible
named after women. One of them is named for a kind girl named Ruth.

Ruth was from a place called Moab. Most of the people in Moab
did not pray to or obey God. But Ruth loved God. She cared about
other people. She cared about her mother-in-law, Naomi.

Many sad things happened to Ruth and Naomi. Naomi's husband
died. Then Ruth's husband died. Ruth and Naomi were left alone.
Sometimes they did not have enough food to eat. One day Ruth said,
"Mother Naomi, I am going to a farm down the road. After they pick
the grain maybe I can get some that is dropped on the ground. Then
we will have something to eat."

So Ruth walked down to the farm. The
owner of the farm was nice to her. "You
can have all the leftover grain," he said.
"We will also share our water with you."

Ruth told her sad mother-in-law how
the people shared with her. Naomi said,
"God still cares about us."

No matter what happens, whether we
are sad or hungry or alone, God still cares
about us. Nothing can stop God from loving you and me.

Questions:
1. What is the name of the kind girl in
this story? (Ruth)
2. Who cares about us no matter what happens? (God)

Activities:
1. Name people God cares about (examples: Grandma _____,
Uncle _____, Daddy, me).
2. For extended activity: Take a walk to a field and talk about how
Ruth picked up leftover grain so she could make flour and then bread.

Prayer:
Dear God, thank You that no matter where I am You never stop
loving and caring about me. Amen.

NAOMI SMILES AGAIN
RUTH 3, 4

Trust in God! I shall again praise him for his wondrous help;
he will make me smile again.
Psalm 43:5 (The Living Bible)

Who went to the fields each day to pick up the leftover grain? Yes, Ruth did. All the farm workers shared with her. But Boaz, the owner of the farm was the most kind. Ruth was kind to Boaz, too. He liked her. And she liked him. They decided to get married.

After awhile Ruth and Boaz had a baby. "It's a boy!" shouted Naomi. "I'm a grandmother!" God had given Naomi a grandson. God helped sad Naomi to smile again.

Naomi held her baby grandson in her arms. She hugged and kissed him. She rocked him. She changed his clothes. She wrapped him in soft blankets. The baby was quiet and cuddly in Grandma Naomi's arms.

_____, can you point to Grandma Naomi in the picture? She was happy because her grandson's birth meant the family name would keep going on. Many years later, Jesus was born from the relatives of Ruth and her baby boy.

Questions:
1. Who did Ruth marry? (Boaz, the owner of the farm)
2. Who had a baby? (Ruth and Boaz)
3. Who was the baby's grandma? (Naomi)

Activities:
1. Pretend to hold a new baby in your arms.
2. Find pictures in a magazine of babies or grandmas and babies. (Or look at pictures of your child and her grandma.)

Prayer:
Dear God, You helped sad Naomi to smile again. You loved and cared about her. Thank you for loving and caring about my grandma. And thank You for loving and caring about me. Amen.

SAMUEL IS BORN
1 SAMUEL 1:9-20

God listens to us every time we ask Him.
1 John 5:15

_____, God brought you into our family _____ years ago. We were so happy to have you to love and hold. We watched you grow.

Hannah wanted a baby to love, hold, and watch grow. She and her husband had no children. "I will go to the tabernacle-church to pray to God. He will help me," she thought. Tears came down her cheeks as she prayed, "Oh, Lord, I am very sad. Would You please give me a son? If you let me have a baby boy, I will give him back to You. Then he can serve You all his life."

God heard Hannah's prayer.  He decided that it would be a good idea for Hannah and her husband to have a baby boy. It was a happy day when Hannah found out she would have a baby. The baby grew inside of her. She waited nine long months. Finally, the day came.

"A boy, I have a baby boy!" said Hannah. "I will call him Samuel." The name, Samuel, means "God heard." Hannah gave her baby this name to remind her that God answered her prayer.

Questions:
1. Who wanted a baby very much? (Hannah)
2. What did Hannah name her baby boy? (Samuel)

Activities:
1. Make a sad face. Make a happy face.
2. Look through magazines for pictures of mothers and babies together. Cut them out and attach them to a sheet of paper. Write: Mommy loves _____ (name of child) on the page with the pictures. (Adjust this activity to fit your specific circumstances.)

Prayer:
Dear God, Hannah loved Samuel. Thank You that Mom and Dad love me. Hannah prayed to You. Thank You that we can pray, also. Amen.

SAMUEL WAVES GOOD-BYE
1 SAMUEL 1:21-28

All you who put your hope in the Lord be strong and brave.
Psalm 31:24

Hannah loved her son, Samuel. She talked and played with him. She taught him to obey. Maybe she told him about her promise and prayer to God. Hannah liked being Samuel's mother.

"Samuel, let's pack your bags," said Hannah one day. "It's time to go to the tabernacle-church. Eli, the priest, is going to take care of you. You will stay with him and help him."

Finally, Hannah and her family got to the tabernacle-church. Hannah brought Samuel to Eli. "I am the sad woman who prayed to God for a son," said Hannah. "God said yes to me. He turned my sadness to joy. Now I give (dedicate) my son, Samuel, to God for as long as he lives."

Hannah believed God would take care of her little son. She knew that God had a very special job for Samuel. Little Samuel stood beside Eli and waved good-bye. Maybe his mother's prayers helped Samuel have courage to believe that God would take care of him in his new home.

Just like Samuel, God will take care of you, _____, wherever you go.

Questions:

1. Where did Samuel and his family go? (They went to the tabernacle-church.)

2. Who did Samuel stay with? (Eli, the priest)

Activities:

1. Play a quiet game together with your child (idea: throw a small ball back and forth).

2. Hug your child and say, "I love you."

Prayer:

Dear God, Hannah kept her promise to You. I want to keep my promises, too. Help me to be strong and believe that You will take care of me even when Mom and Dad are not with me. Amen.

SAMUEL: GOD'S HELPER
1 SAMUEL 2:11, 18-21, 26; 3:1-10; 10:1

Serve the Lord with all your heart. *Romans 12:11*

_____, are you a helper? Do you know that when you obey and help Mom and Dad that you are also helping God? Little Samuel was a helper. The Bible says he helped the Lord. Samuel worked with Eli, the priest, in the tabernacle-church where he lived.

One night while sleeping, he heard a voice say, "Samuel, Samuel." Samuel ran to Eli. "Here I am. What do you want?"

"I did not call you, Samuel," answered Eli. "Go back to sleep."

So Samuel climbed back into bed and closed his eyes. "Samuel," he heard again. He jumped out of bed the second time and ran to Eli. "I

did not call you," said Eli. "Go lie down."

"Samuel," called the voice a third time. Again, Samuel ran to Eli. This time Eli said, "I think the Lord is calling you, Samuel. If He calls again, tell Him you are listening."

When he went back to bed, Samuel heard the voice once more. "Yes, Lord," answered Samuel. "What do You want to tell me?" And Samuel listened to the words of the Lord.

Samuel became God's special messenger. As a grown-up, Samuel was God's prophet. A prophet tells people the words of God. One day God said to Samuel, "A man named Saul is going to be the king. I want you to tell the people." So Samuel obeyed God just like he did when he was a little boy.

Questions:
1. Who helped Eli and the Lord? (Samuel)
2. Who called Samuel in the night? (God)

Activity:
Name ways that Samuel may have helped Eli (ideas: sweeping the floor, greeting people, putting oil in the lamps).

Prayer:
Dear God, I want to be a helper just like Samuel. Please help me. I will listen to Your words in the Bible. Amen.

GOD LOOKS INSIDE
1 SAMUEL 15—16:13

People look at the outside of a person,
but the Lord looks at the heart. *1 Samuel 16:7*

Saul was the new king of the people. "God will help you," Samuel said. "Listen to Him. Do what He says." But Saul made up his mind to disobey God. He started to think that he did not need God's help.

One day God came to Samuel and said, "Saul no longer obeys me, so I am choosing a new king for the people. Go to Bethlehem. The new king lives there. I will show you who he is."

So Samuel did what God said. He took a trip to Bethlehem. Then he went to the house of a man with eight sons. The man's name was Jesse. First, Samuel met Jesse's son, Eliab. He was tall and handsome. Samuel thought this son must be the one to be king.

But God said, "No, Samuel, he is not the new king. You think he looks like he would be a good king. But I have not chosen him. People look at the outside of a person, but God looks at the heart."

Samuel met seven of Jesse's sons. Each time God said, "No, he's not the one."

"I have only one more son," said Jesse. "I will go get him." So Jesse's youngest son came inside to meet Samuel.

Then God said, "Yes, this is the one I want to be the new king." This eighth son of Jesse was named David. God looked at David's heart. He saw that he was kind and good and that David wanted to obey Him.

_____, we cannot tell by what someone looks like on the outside whether they love God. Only God knows that.

Questions:

1. Why did God tell Samuel that He was going to choose a new king? (because Saul had decided to disobey God)

2. Who did God choose to be the new king? (David)

Activity:

Count to eight.

Prayer:

Dear God, thank You that You look inside of me, at my heart, and not at what I'm wearing or what my hair looks like. Amen.

DAVID SINGS FOR KING SAUL
1 SAMUEL 16:14-23

Praise him with harps. *Psalm 150:3*

_____, do you like music and singing? What is your favorite musical instrument?

King Saul liked music. When King Saul was sad, listening to music helped him feel better.

Saul was worried. He was sad and mad. He was not feeling good. His servant-helpers wanted to help him feel better.

"Maybe music will make King Saul happy," his servant-helpers said. "Let's find someone who plays a musical instrument and has a beautiful singing voice."

Saul thought the servant-helpers' idea was a very good one. "Bring some music to me," he said. "Music will make me feel better." (This was a long time ago. There were no radios or televisions. There were no record players or videos.)

One servant-helper said, "Jesse has a son who plays the harp. He is very good. I will ask him to come play for the king."

So Jesse's son, David, sang and played for Saul. Saul loved David's music! And Saul liked David, too. Saul asked David to be his special helper. Whenever King Saul was sad or worried, he called David. And when David played his harp, Saul felt better.

King Saul did not know it, but God had chosen David to be the next king. God was getting David ready for his new job as king of His people.

Questions:

1. Who did not feel good? (King Saul)
2. Who came to sing and play for King Saul? (David)
3. What did David play? (a harp)
4. Did David's music help King Saul feel better? (yes)

Activities:

1. Name musical instruments (ideas: piano, drums, guitar, trumpet, flute).
2. If you have access to a musical instrument, let your child see it, listen to it, or play it.

Prayer:

Dear God, You made music. Thank You for "singing" and "playing." It sounds so pretty. Amen.

DAVID IS A SHEPHERD
1 SAMUEL 17:12-30

I trust in God. I will not be afraid.
What can people do to me? *Psalm 56:11*

_____, what sound does a sheep make? Yes. "Ba-a-a!" is what sheep and lambs say.

David heard this sound every day. David was a shepherd. A shepherd takes care of many sheep. David was the shepherd for his father's sheep.

One day David's father, Jesse, walked out to see him with the sheep.

"David," said his father, "your brothers are away from home now. They are fighting a war with King Saul. Please take this food to them. Then come back and tell me how they are."

So David got another shepherd to take care of his sheep. Then he left to go see his brothers. His oldest brother was not glad to see him. He was mean to David. "You should not be here. Go home and take care of the sheep," he said.

But David was not afraid of what his brother said. David knew God was with him. God had a very special job for David to do. When God has a special job for us to do, we do not have to be afraid of what other people say.

Questions:
1. What is a person called who takes care of sheep? (a shepherd)
2. What did David's father ask him to do? (take food to his brothers who were fighting a war with King Saul)
3. Was David's oldest brother glad to see him? (no)

Activities:
1. Make a sound like a sheep or lamb.
2. Make a cotton-ball sheep. Draw a picture of a lamb. Then glue cotton balls to the picture.

Prayer:
Dear God, David was not afraid when his brother was mean to him. He was not afraid because he knew You would help him. Help me, too, when people are mean to me. Amen.

DAVID AND THE GIANT
1 SAMUEL 17:1-11, 26-51

But where does my help come from?
My help comes from the Lord. *Psalm 121:1, 2*

_____, do you know what a giant is? A giant is a very big person. Goliath was nine feet, four inches tall.

Goliath was fighting against King Saul, David's brothers, and all Saul's soldiers. Goliath had soldiers with him, too. But Goliath and his soldiers did not know God. They did not believe God. They made fun of Saul and his soldiers. Saul's soldiers were afraid of Goliath.

David said, "Why does Goliath think he can make fun of God and God's soldiers?" Then David talked to King Saul. "Don't worry," he told Saul. "I will fight Goliath for you."

King Saul said, "David, you are a good singer. I like your music. But you are only a boy. How can you fight Goliath? He's so big."

"I am a shepherd," said David. "I killed a bear and a lion when they hurt my sheep. God helped me do that, and He will help me with Goliath, too."

So David got five small smooth rocks and his special slingshot. Then he walked up to the bad giant, Goliath. Goliath made fun of David. But David said, "God is with me." So David put a small smooth rock in his slingshot and threw it at Goliath. The rock hit Goliath, and he crashed to the ground.

David was not afraid of Goliath, because God helped him.

Questions:
   1. What was the giant's name? (Goliath)
   2. Did Goliath know and believe God? (no)
   3. Who helped David? (God)

Activity:
   Measure how tall your child is. Measure how tall you are.

Prayer:
   Dear God, You helped David. I know You can help me, too, even when something seems too hard for me to do. Thank You. Amen.

FRIENDS FOREVER
1 SAMUEL 18:1-16, 28-30; 19:1-7; 20:1-42

A friend loves you all the time.
(He) is always there to help you. *Proverbs 17:17*

King Saul had a son. His name was Jonathan. Jonathan and David became very good friends. They spent lots of time together. _____, do you like to do things with your friends? David and Jonathan liked to do things together, too.

Do you remember when David fought the fight against the giant, Goliath? After that, King Saul asked David to be a soldier. David was a very good soldier. He helped King Saul's army with lots of battles. All the people liked him. But soon King Saul became jealous. He wanted all the people to think that he alone was the best soldier. He did not want people to like David. He did not want people to talk about David so much.

But Jonathan was different than his father, King Saul. He was not jealous. He really loved David. He was happy that the people liked David. Jonathan knew that God was with David. He believed God. He knew that David would someday be the king. He helped David get away from the jealous King Saul. Jonathan was a real friend to David.

We can be a good friend, too. When our friends are sad or sick or having trouble, we can help them.

Questions:
1. What was King Saul's son's name? (Jonathan)
2. Who were very good friends? (David and Jonathan)
3. Who was jealous of David? (King Saul)
4. Did Jonathan help his friend David? (yes)

Activities:
1. Name your friends.
2. Write a note or draw a picture for a friend. Mail it.

Prayer:
Dear God, thank You for my friends. Help me to be a good and kind friend. Amen.

FRIENDS PRAY FOR EACH OTHER
1 SAMUEL 18:1-4; 20:42

I thank God every time I remember you. And I always pray for you.
Philippians 1:3, 4

Bobby and Richie were good friends. They played ball together. They had lunch together. They even went to preschool together. Every day they were with each other. If Bobby got sick, Richie was sad. If Richie was sick, Bobby was sad. They were very special friends.

One day Richie's dad said he was going to take a job in a far away city. The family would have to move. So Richie told Bobby the news. Richie and Bobby were sad. They knew they would miss each other very much.

"What should we do?" they thought.

"Maybe we can pray to God about how we feel," said Richie. "He knows we are sad. I think He will help us."

"Dear God," Bobby prayed, "please help us when we say good-bye to each other. You know that we are sad because we won't be able to play together anymore. Help Richie to meet friends in his new city. And help me here. Thank You. Amen."

A long time ago, David and Jonathan were special friends, too. God gives us friends. We can pray to God about our friends.

Questions:
1. Who were very special friends? (Bobby and Richie)
2. Who had to move to a far away city? (Richie)
3. Were Richie and Bobby sad? (yes)
4. What did Bobby and Richie do? (They prayed to God for help.)

Activities:
1. Name your friends.
2. Ask a friend to come over and play.

Prayer:
Dear God, thank You for my friend, _____. Please help him(her) today. Amen.

DAVID PRAYED
1 SAMUEL 23:14,15; 2 SAMUEL 2:1; 5:23; 7:18

But I pray to you, Lord. *Psalm 69:13*

_____, when you decide about something, you make up your mind. Sometimes you decide where to go or what to wear or what to eat. David had lots of decisions to make. David prayed to God when he needed to make a decision.

The jealous King Saul chased after David all over the country. It was a hard and scary time for David. One time soldiers came to take David's family away. David cried. He prayed, and God helped him get his family back.

After Saul died, David asked God if he should move. God said, "Yes." So David moved to a place called Judah. The people there made him king. Then David became the king of Israel. He was king for 40 years. That was a long time.

David knew that it was God's idea for him to be king. When the other kings and countries heard that David was the king of Israel, they came to fight him.

"What should I do?" whispered David. So he prayed to God. Whatever God told him to do, he did. When God said, "Go," David went. David loved God very much.

We show God we love Him by praying to Him and by doing what He says to do. We can pray to God when we are at home or church; at school or on the playground. God is ready to hear us and to answer our prayers anytime.

Questions:
1. Who prayed to God? (David)
2. David became king of what two countries? (first Judah and then Israel)
3. Whose plan was it for David to be king? (God's)

Activities:
1. Name times you have to decide.
2. Make a king's crown out of 8" x 11" paper. Color it and then glue or staple it together. Wear it.

Prayer:
Dear God, please help me today as I decide about _____. Thank You. Amen. (Fill in the blank with a specific prayer need that you have.)

GOD SAYS "NO"
2 SAMUEL 7:1-29

Lord God, your words are true. And you
have promised these good things to me. *2 Samuel 7:28*

David was the king. He lived in a big and beautiful home called a palace. There was no fighting in the place where he was king. The fighting was over. It was peace time.

One day, David said, "I want to build God a big, beautiful building."

That same night, God talked to a prophet-man named Nathan. God said, "Nathan, tell David these words: 'I have always been with you. I have helped you. I took the fighting away. I made peace time for you now. When you are gone, your son will become the next king. *He* is the one who will build the new building for me. Remember, I will never stop loving you or your family.'"

King David wanted to build a beautiful building for God. God said, "No." But that was alright with David, because God had promised that David's son could build the building. David loved God. He wanted to do just what God told him to do.

"I know that You will keep Your promise to me and to my son. You are God. Your words are always true," David prayed.

_____, God always hears and answers our prayers. Sometimes He answers right away; sometimes He says wait a while. Sometimes His answer is "No." His answer to David about the building was "No." God had a different plan, but He always keeps His promises.

Questions:

1. Who wanted to build a building for God? (King David)

2. Did God want David to build the building? (no)

3. Who did God want to build the building? (David's son)

Activity:

Build a tall building with your blocks (or stack boxes or books).

Prayer:

Dear God, thank You for always answering me. What You promise will come true. I believe You. Amen.

THE SMARTEST KING
1 KINGS 1:1-52; 3:1-15; 2 CHRONICLES 1:7-12

But if any of you needs wisdom, you should ask God for it.
James 1:5

_____, Solomon was one of King David's many sons. God told David that Solomon would be the next King. So David said, "Blow the trumpet. Shout the news! Solomon is king."

Solomon was a good king. He loved God. One night, God came to him and said, "Ask me for anything, and I promise to give it to you."

Solomon was a young man. He was strong and good looking. He was the leader of many people. He could have asked God for lots of money, new clothes, a bigger house, the best chariots. But he did not. He could have asked God to let him live a long time without getting sick or old. But he did not. He could have asked God to get rid of all the other kings and countries that did not like him. But he did not. Solomon did not ask for any of these things.

"Lord, my God," Solomon said. "You are the one who let me be king over all these people. But I cannot do a good job unless You help me. So I ask You for wisdom. I ask that You help me to make smart, good decisions. I ask that You tell me how to help all these people. Please help me to know what is right and what is wrong."

God was happy with what Solomon said. "I will give you wisdom. You will be smarter than any other man," said God. "Now, Solomon, I ask you to obey me. Do this just like your father, David, did."

Solomon became the wisest man who ever lived. It was God who gave him his wisdom.

Questions:
1. Who was the new king? (David's son, Solomon)
2. What did Solomon ask for and receive from God? (wisdom)

Activity:
Draw a picture of the new king, Solomon.

Prayer:
Dear God, please help me to make smart decisions. Help me to know what is right and what is wrong. Amen.

JASON'S BIRTHDAY
PROVERBS 8:1-35; 1 KINGS 3:1-15

Wisdom begins with respect for the Lord. Proverbs 9:10

Jason was five years old on his birthday. He got a new TV from his mom and dad and a new bike from his grandparents. He also got new clothes and a pair of special shoes. He had lots of nice new things.

At dinner, Jason said, "I don't like the new kid at our school. He has ugly clothes. And he has an old bike."

Mom tucked Jason in bed that night. "Jason," she said. "I want to talk to you. It seems you think that because you have new clothes and lots of nice things that you are better than other children. I'm thankful for your new TV and bike, but there is something more important than money and new things. It is more important to love God and to ask His help in making good, smart decisions. King Solomon knew this, even though he had lots of nice things. God helped Solomon to be wise. You think about it." Mom kissed Jason. "I love you," she said.

Soon Jason fell asleep. He dreamed that his house caught fire. His new TV and bike were burned. His clothes and shoes were gone. He was very sad. In the morning when he woke up, he was so happy that it was only a dream. But it made him think.

"Dear God," he said, "I know that You are more important than anything else I have. Please help me to remember that. Amen."

_____, Jason made a smart decision. He made up his mind to pray to God for help. He decided that God was more important than his toys and new things.

Questions:
1. Who had lots of nice new things? (Jason)
2. What did Jason tell God after his dream? (You are more important than anything else.)

Activity:
Name some things that are important to God (ideas: love, kindness; obedience; prayer; making smart decisions; telling the truth).

Prayer:
Dear God, please help me to make good, smart decisions about what I do and think. Amen.

GOD'S HOUSE
1 KINGS 6:1-38

I was happy when they said to me,
"Let's go to the Temple of the Lord." *Psalm 122:1*

King David wanted to build a beautiful building for God. But God said, "No, David, your son is the one who will build the building for me." Before David died, he taught his teenage son, Solomon, how to build the building. God called the building a "temple." It was to be like a church building. It was going to be beautiful and very special.

After Solomon had been king for four years, he started to build the temple. Many people helped. There was a front porch. And there was a special room called the "Most Holy Place." The ten special rules (or commandments) that Moses got from God were kept in this special room. It took Solomon and all the workers seven years to build the temple-church.

This special temple was God's house. The people worshipped God in this temple-church. They sang and prayed to God. We can worship God when we go to church, too. We can sing and talk to God.

_____, aren't you happy when you get to go to church and sing and learn about God?

Questions:
1. How long did it take to build the temple? (seven years)
2. Whose house was it? (God's house)

Activities:
1. Count to seven. (It took seven years to build the temple.)
2. Draw a picture of the church you attend.

Prayer:
Dear God, I am happy when I get to go to church and learn about You. But I know that I can pray to You even when I'm not at church. Thank You for listening to me. Amen.

JIMMY GETS READY FOR CHURCH
PSALM 147:1-9; 1 KINGS 6:1-38

Let them praise his greatness in the meeting of the people.
Psalm 107:32

_____, it's fun to go to church school, isn't it? We can sing and talk about Jesus there. And it's fun to see our friends. Jimmy liked to go to church school, too.

One morning, he woke up early. It was church day. He climbed out of bed very quietly. He did not want to wake up his mom and dad yet. He tiptoed to the kitchen. He ate a bowl of cereal. Then he brushed his teeth and washed his face and hands. He walked back to his room.

"What should I wear to church?" he thought. "I'll surprise Mom and Dad and get dressed all by myself."

He reached into his drawer for a red sweater. That looked nice with his gray pants. Jimmy pulled on a pair of socks. Then he tried to tie the laces on his good black shoes. It was very hard. He tried again and again. Finally, he did it! He was so happy that he clapped his hands.

"I thought I heard you in here," said Dad as he peeked in Jimmy's room. Then Dad saw that Jimmy was all dressed. "Oh, my, you look very nice."

"I'm ready to go to church," said Jimmy. "I want to go sing my songs to God."

We like to go sing songs of praise to God, too, don't we? We can praise God at church. We can also praise God at home.

Questions:
1. Where did Jimmy like to go? (church school)
2. What did Jimmy do at church? (sing, talk about Jesus, see friends)

Activities:
1. Try to tie your shoes.
2. Sing a song of praise to God.

Prayer:
Dear God, I like to sing songs of praise to You. You are very great. Amen.

THE PEOPLE CHANGED
1 KINGS 17:1-16

Do not change yourselves to be like the people of this world.
Romans 12:2

God stayed the same, but the people changed. They did not want to sing and pray to God anymore. They decided to sing and pray to wooden and stone gods (like statues). It was not a wise decision. The people had lots of bad leaders. The leaders were kings who did not love God. God did so many wonderful things for the people. But they did not care. They did not say thank You. They did not love God. It made God sad and even mad.

So God sent a prophet-man named Elijah to talk to the king. His name was Ahab. King Ahab did not love God. But Elijah loved God. He did what God told him to do. Elijah said, "King Ahab, God says there will be no rain for the next few years."

_____, what happens when there is no rain? When there is no rain, plants, trees, and vegetables die. When there is no rain, animals and people do not have water to drink because the lakes all dry up. (This is called a drought.) The drought was hard for all the people. The people did not have enough food to eat.

But God made a way for Elijah to have food and water during the drought. God took care of him. Elijah loved and prayed to God even in the hard times. He did not change his mind about God like the people did. God wants us to keep believing Him. We can decide that we will never change our minds about loving God.

Questions:
1. Who changed their minds about loving God? (the people)
2. What did Elijah tell King Ahab? (There will be no rain for a few years.)
3. Did Elijah change his mind about loving God? (no)
4. Did God take care of Elijah during the drought? (Yes. God gave Elijah food and water.)

Activity:
Water the plants or garden together.
Prayer:
Dear God, Elijah did not change his mind about loving and believing You. Even when it is hard, I want to keep loving You. Amen.

MY SON IS ALIVE!
1 KINGS 17:8-24

God can do all things. *Matthew 19:26*

When the rain stopped and the lakes dried up, Elijah wondered where he would get water to drink and food to eat. But God took care of him. "Go live in a different city," God said. "I know a lady who will help you." So Elijah obeyed.

After his long walk to the other city, he was hungry and thirsty. "May I please have a drink of water and a piece of bread?" he asked a lady standing near him.

"I don't have any bread," she answered. "I'm telling you the truth. My son and I will soon die from hunger, because we only have a little bit of flour and olive oil."

"Don't worry," Elijah said. "God is going to fill up your flour and oil jars. All three of us will have enough food to eat." Elijah went home with the lady and stayed in a room on the roof of her house. And God gave them food to eat.

One day the lady's son got very sick and died. "Elijah, you are God's prophet-man," the sad mother cried. "Do you know why my son died?"

Elijah felt sorry for the mother. "Give your son to me," he said. Elijah carried the boy up the stairs to his room and put him on the bed. Elijah prayed, "Oh, Lord God, please make this boy alive again."

Suddenly the boy opened his eyes. He hugged his mother. "My son is alive!" she shouted. "I know that God is with you, Elijah."

God helped Elijah do something wonderful. It was a miracle!

Questions:
1. Where did Elijah stay? (in a room on the roof)
2. Who helped Elijah make the boy alive again? (God)

Activity:
Walk your fingers up your child's arm. Say, "Elijah climbed the stairs up to his room."

Prayer:
Dear God, no one is like You. You can do wonderful things. Amen.

WHERE DID ELIJAH GO?
1 KINGS 19:19-21; 2 KINGS 2:1-15

But the Holy Spirit will come to you. Then you will receive power.

Acts 1:8

_____, who was the prophet-man of God whose name started with an "E"? Yes, his name was Elijah. Elijah did what God asked him to do. But he was getting old. Who would do God's work when Elijah was gone?

One day when Elijah was walking he came to a field. A man named Elisha worked there. (The names Elijah and Elisha sound alike, don't they?) Elijah took off his coat and put it on Elisha. He did this to show that he wanted to call Elisha to be his helper. Right away, Elisha stopped working. He decided to follow God for the rest of his life.

One day as Elijah and Elisha walked together, they came to a river. Elijah hit the river water with his coat. Immediately, God divided the water in the river. It made a dry road for the two men to walk on.

"Elijah, please give me some of your God-given power," said Elisha.

"God is the one who gives power to do miracles. But if you watch me when I go to heaven, then you will have God's power, too."

Then something very different happened! God sent special horses and chariots to come get Elijah. One minute Elijah stood beside Elisha. And the next minute Elijah went to heaven with wind whirling around him. Soon Elisha found out that God had given him power to do miracles, just as Elijah said He would.

Questions:

1. What were the names of the two men? (Elijah and Elisha)

2. Where did Elijah go? (to heaven in a whirling wind)

Activities:

1. Think of names that sound similar (examples: Joan and Jean, Rich and Rick, Pat and Matt).

2. Plan to take a walk together.

Prayer:

Dear God, thank You for giving us power to do the things that we cannot do by ourselves. Amen.

GO AWAY, BALDHEAD!
2 KINGS 2:23-25

If you make fun of the poor, you insult God, who made them.
Proverbs 17:5

_____, have you ever heard children call out mean names to another child? How do you think that little child feels when someone makes fun of him? He might feel sad or hurt or embarrassed or even mad.

One day, many, many years ago, some young men made fun of the prophet, Elisha. "Get out of here, Baldhead! Go away!" they yelled at Elisha. When these young men made fun of Elisha, they were really making fun of God. Elisha was God's special man. When they called mean names to Elisha, they were calling mean names to God. This was a very bad thing to do. The young men's actions showed that they did not care about or believe in God at all.

We would never want to say mean things to God. But when we make fun of any of God's children, it makes God sad. Let's remember this. It is not good to make fun of children who are different than we are.

Questions:
1. Who made fun of Elisha? (some young men)
2. What did they call Elisha? (baldhead)
3. Who were they really making fun of? (God)
4. Is God unhappy when we make fun of others? (yes)

Activity:
Name ways that children can be different from other children (ideas: One is very tall or very short or fat. One may have ears that stick out or a hand that does not work right.).

Prayer:
Dear God, I do not want to make fun of other children. I know that is not a kind thing to do. Please help me to remember that. Thank You. Amen.

A SILLY IDEA?
2 KINGS 5:1-14

There is no God in all the earth except in Israel! 2 Kings 5:15

Naaman was an important leader. Many people thought he was great because his army won lots of fights. But one day he got sick. He had a bad skin disease. It was called leprosy. Naaman wanted to get well, but people with this sickness only became worse.

Now Naaman had a young girl who worked for him. She knew about the prophet-man Elisha. "I wish my master would go see Elisha. He would make him well," she said. So Naaman decided to go see Elisha.

Naaman found Elisha's house and knocked on the door. Elisha sent his helper out to see Naaman. The helper said, "Go to the Jordan River. Wash off seven times in the river. Then you will be well."

This made Naaman mad. "I don't like the Jordan River. It's dirty! And besides that, I don't want Elisha's helper to talk to me. I want Elisha!" So Naaman stomped away.

But Naaman's own helpers tried to talk to him. "Calm down," they said. "You came all this way. At least *try* what he says to do."

So Naaman walked down and splashed in the river. 1—2—3 times, but nothing happened. 4—5—6 times. "This is silly!" he thought. But when he came out of the water the seventh time, he was well!

Then Naaman said, "Now I believe in God."

_____, God helped Elisha make Naaman well again. It was another miracle.

Questions:
1. Who had a bad skin disease? (Naaman)
2. Where did Elisha tell Naaman to go wash? (in the Jordan River)
3. Did Naaman think it was a silly idea? (yes)

Activity:
Pretend to wash off seven times in the river.

Prayer:
Dear God, You helped Elisha to do special things. It shows that You are very powerful. Amen.

THE BOY KING
2 CHRONICLES 34:1-13; 35:26

Remember your Creator while you are young.
Ecclesiastes 12:1

The Jewish people had many different kings. Most of them did not love God. But one king made up his mind to do what God said. His name was Josiah.

Josiah became king when he was only eight years old. He was very young to be a king. But Josiah made an important decision. He said, "I am just a child. But I can pray and sing to God. I want to love God just like my great-grandfather, King David."

So Josiah told his helpers to get rid of all the false statue gods. He broke the statues and then threw them away. Then he decided to fix the temple-church of God. For many years the bad kings let the temple-church get dirty and broken. It made God very sad. But Josiah changed all that.

Josiah loved the Lord God. He became king when he was very young, but he never forgot God. He knew that God created and loved him. He believed all of God's words.

_____, how old are you? You are young like Josiah. God created you, too. He loves you. He wants you to remember that.

Questions:
1. Did most of the Jewish kings love God? (no)
2. Who became a king when he was eight years old? (Josiah)
3. Did Josiah love the Lord God? (yes)

Activities:
1. Count to eight.
2. Make a crown out of heavy paper. Pretend to be a king.

Prayer:
Dear God, I am ____ years old now, but I am growing. I will remember that You made me and that You love me. Amen.

DANIEL'S DECISION
DANIEL 1:1-21

Daniel decided not to eat the king's food
because that would make him unclean. *Daniel 1:8*

_____, a long time ago there was a king with a very long name. His name was Ne-bu-chad-nez-zar. One day the king asked his helper, Ashpenaz, to do a special job for him.

"Go and find the smartest, strongest, best-looking young Israelite men you can find," he said. "I want them to come study, train, and eat like me for three years. At the end of the three years of school, they will work for me."

So the king's helper found a group of special men. One young man was named Daniel. Daniel loved God. He wanted to do what made God happy. Daniel believed that God did not want him to eat the king's food. So Daniel made a brave decision. He said, "Please don't make me eat this food."

But the king's helper was afraid. "We must obey the king, or he'll cut off my head," he said.

Then Daniel had an idea. He explained it to the king's helper. "I have three friends who love God, too. Let all four of us eat *our* food for ten days. The other young men can eat the *king's* food for ten days. At the end of that time you decide who is the strongest and healthiest."

After the ten days, Daniel and his friends were healthier than the other young men. So Ashpenaz let Daniel and his friends eat their food for the next three years. God helped these four young men. They did very well in the king's school. When the three years were over, they went to work for King Nebuchadnezzar. Daniel was very brave to do what he felt was the right thing.

Questions:
1. Who made a brave decision? (Daniel)
2. Who helped the four young men? (God)

Activity:
Say Ne-bu-chad-nez-zar.

Prayer:
Dear God, help me to make brave decisions like Daniel did. Amen.

NOT ONE LITTLE BURN!
DANIEL 3:1-30

Don't be afraid when you walk through fire,
you will not be burned. *Isaiah 43:1, 2*

After Nebuchadnezzar was king for awhile, he decided to make a big statue. It was made out of gold. It was 90 feet high. That is as high as ten rooms stacked on top of each other. That's very tall, isn't it, _____?

The king said, "All people everywhere, do what I say. When you hear the music, you must bow down, worship, and pray to the gold statue. Anyone who does not bow down will be quickly thrown into a fiery-hot furnace."

But there were three men who were not afraid. Their names were Shadrach, Meshach, and Abednego. "Our God will help us," they said. "If he saves us from the fire, that is good. But even if He does not, we will not serve your false gods."

So King Nebuchadnezzar made the fiery furnace seven times hotter than before. He tied up the three brave men and threw them into the furnace.

Later, when the king looked into the furnace, he could not believe his eyes! There were *four*, not three, men walking around. An angel of God walked with them. And not one of them had even one little burn! They were safe. It was a miracle. God did something no one else could.

Questions:
1. Who made a 90 foot statue? (King Nebuchadnezzar)
2. Who did not worship and pray to the statue? (Shadrach, Meshach, and Abednego)

Activity:
Name ways that we use fire (ideas: heat the house; cook food, melt metal). Nebuchadnezzar used fire in a bad way.

Prayer:
Dear God, I know that You will always take care of me, on earth or in heaven. Thank You. Amen.

DANIEL AND THE LIONS
DANIEL 6:1-26

He (Daniel) prayed and thanked God, just as he always had done.

Daniel 6:10

_____, can you make a sound like a lion? G-r-r-r! Listen while I tell you a story about Daniel and the lions.

There was a new king in Babylon. His name was King Darius. Daniel was an important leader in King Darius' kingdom. He was the best worker of all. None of the other workers could find anything wrong with him. The king liked him and planned to make him leader of all the others. This made the other workers jealous.

So they decided to trick both Daniel and the king. They told the king to make a new rule. The rule said that if a person prayed to anyone else but King Darius, they would be thrown into the lions' cage. King Darius made this new rule into a law. Nothing could change the law.

Now it was Daniel's habit to pray to God three times each day. He had a special place in his house near a window where he prayed on his knees. Daniel was a brave follower of God. He did not hide just because of the new law. He prayed just like always.

The jealous workers saw him kneeling by his window. They ran to the king and told on Daniel. This made King Darius sad. He liked Daniel very much. But he could not change the law. So into the lions' cage went Daniel. "I hope your God helps you," said the king.

The next morning the king hurried down to the lions' cage. Would Daniel's God help him? He called to Daniel.

"I am OK," Daniel said to the king. "My God sent an angel to close the lions' mouths. They have not hurt me."

King Darius was so happy. His friend and worker, Daniel, was safe. Then he let Daniel out of the lions' cage. King Darius also sent out an order that all people in the kingdom were to worship the God of Daniel.

God helped Daniel, the praying man.

Questions:
1. Who prayed to God three times each day? (Daniel)
2. Who threw Daniel into the lions' cage? (King Darius)

Activity:
Pray to God together on your knees.

Prayer:
Dear God, I will keep praying to You no matter what anyone says. I know You will help me. Amen.

GOOD MORNING, GOD
NEHEMIAH 1:4; 2:4; PSALM 63:1-8

I remember you while I'm lying in bed. *Psalm 63:6*

"LeAnne, call your brother and then come inside," said Tammy. "It's time to get ready for bed." Tammy was the babysitter. Mom and Dad had gone out for the night because it was their anniversary.

So five-year-old LeAnne and three-year-old Donny ran in the house. They put on their favorite pajamas. Donny washed his face and hands. LeAnne brushed her teeth.

"Tammy, will you please read us a bedtime story?" asked Donny.

So Tammy read them a story. Then she turned out the light. "Goodnight," she called, as she walked down the hall. LeAnne thought a minute. Tammy did not pray with them. She and Donny always prayed before they went to sleep What should she do?

LeAnne climbed out of bed and tiptoed to Donny's room. "Psst! Donny, are you asleep?" LeAnne whispered. "Tammy forgot to pray with us. So let's pray together. Just you and me." They prayed together. Soon LeAnne said, "Amen." As she walked out the door, Donny said, "Good night, LeAnne. Good night God."

The next morning when LeAnne opened her eyes, she saw sunlight coming into her window. She heard the birds chirping outside. "Good morning, God," she said, as she jumped out of bed. "Thank You for taking care of me during the night."

LeAnne was like Daniel in the Bible story. She knew it was important to pray to God.

Questions:

1. Who prayed together when Tammy forgot? (LeAnne and Donny)
2. How were LeAnne and Daniel alike? (They both prayed.)

Activity:

If it is bedtime say, "Good night, God." If it is morning say, "Good morning, God."

Prayer:

Dear God, I want to be like Daniel. I will pray to You. Amen.

HIDE-AND-SEEK
JONAH 1:1-16

"No one can hide where I cannot see him," says the Lord.
Jeremiah 23:24

_____, have you ever wanted to run away when Mom or Dad called you? It's not a good idea, is it? Jonah ran away when God called him. It was not a good idea for Jonah, either.

"Jonah," God said, "I want you to go to the very big city of Nineveh. Go there and tell the people to stop doing bad things."

But Jonah acted like he did not hear God. He ran away. He went to the city of Joppa instead of Nineveh. In Joppa he saw a boat. "If I can get on this boat, I can hide from God," he thought. "He won't see me. He won't find me. And then He won't ask me to talk to the mean people of Nineveh."

Soon after the boat sailed into the water, a big storm came. The wind blew so hard it almost broke the ship. The sailor-men were afraid. "Why did this storm come?" they asked.

"It's because of me. I thought I could hide from God," said Jonah. "Throw me into the water." When they threw Jonah into the water, the rain and wind stopped. Then all the sailor-men believed in God.

Jonah thought he could hide from God, but he was wrong. No one can hide from God. God was with the sailors in the boat. God was with Jonah swimming in the water. And God is with you and me reading this story right now.

Questions:
1. Who tried to hide from God? (Jonah)
2. Where did Jonah go to run away from God? (He got on a boat.)

Activities:
1. Pretend your bed or chair is a rocking boat.
2. Play hide-and-seek.

Prayer:
Dear God, Jonah could not hide from You. I cannot hide from You. I'm glad because it means that You always see and help me. Thank You. Amen.

A VERY B-I-G FISH
JONAH 1:17—3:10

And I will do what I promise. *Jonah 2:9*

Who did the sailor-men throw out of the boat? Do you know what happened to Jonah in the water? A b-i-g fish swam close to him while he was floating in the water. Gulp! The fish swallowed Jonah. But Jonah was OK in the stomach of the big fish for three days and nights. While Jonah was in the fish's stomach he prayed to God.

"I thought I might drown in that water, Lord. The gooey seaweed wrapped around my head. But when I prayed, You heard me and sent a fish to swallow me. Thank You for saving me. I promise to do what You want me to do and go to Nineveh." Then the fish sneezed and out flew Jonah onto the dry beach.

_____, what do you think Jonah looked like after the big fish sneezed him out onto the beach? Maybe his skin looked all wrinkly like yours gets when you take a bath.

This time Jonah did not run away. He obeyed God and went to Nineveh. Jonah told the people to listen and obey God.

The people of Nineveh were sorry that they had forgotten God. "We will stop disobeying and doing mean things. We will listen to God." The king told all the people to pray.

God was pleased that the people of Nineveh changed their minds. Jonah changed his mind, and so did the people of Nineveh.

Questions:
1. How long was Jonah inside the fish? (three days and nights)
2. Did the people of Nineveh listen to Jonah's words? (yes)

Activity:
1. Move your arms and pretend that you're swimming.
2. Play in the bathtub and see if your hands wrinkle up.

Prayer:
Dear God, Jonah changed his mind and obeyed You. The people of Nineveh changed their evil ways and obeyed. You always listen and forgive people when they are sorry for disobeying You. Amen.

I LOVE YOU GOOD AS GOLD
MALACHI 1:2

He (God) said, "I love you with a love that will last forever.
Jeremiah 31:3

"Mom, come here. Quick!" Kevin called from his room. "I goofed."

Kevin's mother hurried down the hallway. When she turned the corner and looked in his room, her eyes opened wide. There on the floor was a broken glass of grape juice. The purple juice was dripping down the wall into a big puddle on the yellow carpeting. "I didn't mean to," said Kevin.

"I know you are sorry, Kevin," said Mom. "But let's hurry now and clean it up before it gets worse."

So Kevin and Mom mopped up the sticky wall and wiped the carpet with a wet rag. "Oh, goodie, it's almost gone," said Kevin. They kept working until they couldn't see the purple juice anymore. Then they sat down on the floor to rest.

Suddenly, Kevin leaned over and hugged his mother's neck. "Mom, I love you good as gold," he said.

_____, it's a good feeling when someone loves and forgives you even when you've "goofed," isn't it? Kevin's mom loved him. She forgave him for taking the grape juice into his room when he knew it was against the rules. God loves and forgives us when we goof, too. It makes us want to say back to Him, "God, I love You good as gold."

Questions:

1. Who spilled the purple juice? (Kevin)
2. Who cleaned it up? (Kevin and Mom)
3. Does God love and forgive us when we "goof"? (yes)

Activity:

1. Tell your child, "I love you good as gold."
2. Have a drink of your favorite juice. (Stay in the kitchen!)

Prayer:

Dear God, thank You for loving and forgiving me even when I goof and go against the rules. Amen.

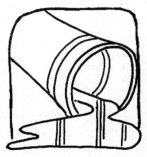

"I LOVE YOU"
MALACHI 1—4

This was written about John in the Scriptures:
"I will send my messenger ahead of you." *Matthew 11:10*

_____, do you like it when someone says, "I love you"? We all like to hear those three little words, don't we?

The last book in the Old Testament (of the Bible) was written by a prophet named Malachi. At the beginning of this book are these three little words: "I love you."

God said these words. God loved His people. But they still did not act like they really loved Him back. It is true that the people had stopped praying to statues and wooden gods (that was good). But they did not do what God said in other things.

What did they do? The men married women who did not pray or sing to God. The church leaders lied and cheated the people. The people took money that belonged to God and spent it on new clothes and bigger houses. And they only half-believed when God's men told them that the Messiah (or Jesus) was going to come.

At the end of the book, Malachi said, "A man like Elijah is going to come." The people remembered Elijah. But who would this new man be? Malachi was talking about John the Baptist. He came 400 years later to tell all people about Jesus. In Matthew, the first book of the New Testament, we read about John the Baptist.

Questions:
1. Who wrote the last book in the Old Testament? (Malachi)
2. Did the people act like they really loved God? (no)
3. Who did Malachi say was going to come? (John the Baptist)

Activity:
1. Whisper these words in your child's ear: "I love you."
2. Find the book of Malachi in the Bible.

Prayer:
Dear God, I know that You loved Your people when Malachi was alive. And I know that You love me now. I love You, too. Amen.